Internal Growth Through Tao

Internal Growth Through Tao

by
Taoist Master
Ni, Hua-Ching

The Shrine of the Eternal Breath of Tao
College of Tao and Traditional Chinese Healing
LOS ANGELES

Acknowledgement: Thanks and appreciation to
Janet DeCourtney and Frank Gibson and the students
of the Center for Taoist Arts for assistance in
typing, proofreading and editing this book.

Shrine of the Eternal Breath of Tao, Malibu, California
College of Tao and Traditional Chinese Healing
117 Stonehaven Way
Los Angeles, CA 90049

This book is dedicated to those
who are working for their
internal spiritual growth,
and live their life in the light.

Prelude

"Tao is the destination of all religions, while it leaves behind all religions just like the clothing of different seasons and different places. Tao is the goal of serious science, but it leaves behind all sciences as a partial and temporal description of the Integral Truth.

"The teaching of Tao includes all religious subjects, yet it is not on the same level as religions. Its breadth and depth go far beyond the limits of religion. The teaching of Tao serves people's lives like religions do, yet it transcends all religions and contains the essence of all religions.

"The teaching of Tao is not like any of the sciences. It is above the level of any single subject of science.

"The teaching of Tao is the master teaching of all. However, it does not mean the teaching relies on a master. It means the teaching of Tao is like a master key which can unlock all doors leading to the Integral Truth. It teaches or shows the truth directly. It does not stay on the emotional surface of life or remain at the level of thought or belief. Neither does it stay on the intellectual level of life, maintaining skepticism and searching endlessly. The teaching of Tao presents the core of the subtle truth and helps you to reach it yourself."

CONTENTS

To female readers,

According to Taoist teaching, male and female are equally important in the natural sphere. This is seen in the diagram of Tai Chi. Thus, discrimination is not practiced in our tradition. All my work is dedicated to both genders of human people.

Wherever possible, constructions using masculine pronouns to represent both sexes are avoided; where they occur, we ask your tolerance and spiritual understanding. We hope that you will take the essence of my teaching and overlook the superficiality of language. Gender discrimination is inherent in English; ancient Chinese pronouns do not have differences of gender. I wish for all of your achievement above the level of language or gender.

Thank you, H. C. Ni

Warning - Disclaimer

This book is intended to present information and techniques that have been in use throughout the orient for many years. The information offered is to the author's best knowledge and experience and is to be used by the reader(s) at their own discretion. The information and practices utilize a natural system within the mind and body, however, there are no claims for their effectiveness. It is not a cure-all like the claims of conventional religions.

Because of the condensed nature of the information contained within this book, it is recommended that the reader of this book also study the author's other books for further knowledge about a healthy lifestyle and energy conducting exercises.

The author and publisher of this book are not responsible in any manner whatsoever for any harm which may occur by misapplication of the instructions in this book.

Preface

The truth is one, the teachings are many.
The heart is one, the minds are numerous.
Religious teachings are the expression of the precious heart energy. Although a thousand people have a thousand different minds, there is only one, similar heart energy. When the precious heart energy is put into performance or demonstration, it is then described by different names, rituals, worships or structures of belief. Those multiple expressions are only representations of the energy of the heart. Aside from the precious energy of heart, what else can you call God?

In a big modern city of a free, open society, there are all kinds of temples and churches which work and teach separately. Their teachings, historical backgrounds, ways, terminologies, and colorful decorations are all different. The differences in expression come from the differences in the minds of the people who do the planning or worshipping.

All different temples, churches and schools of teaching only serve one thing: the heart. People who only go to a regular type of school learn no more than to stretch their intelligence; they learn nothing that connects with the heart. Thus, different types of schools arise to respond to the heart's need.

In ancient times, the Chinese word, "Shing" usually meant the heart, but it also meant the mind. Spiritually, the heart and mind are one in an individual in babyhood and in the earlier stages of life. Later, a separation happens between the heart and the mind of a individual and the society; personal intellect is no longer united with the heart. They go different ways. However, even though they are separate, the heart always wishes to call its partner back to serve the life being together.

The mind disobeys or rebels against the heart. The mind says, "What nonsense you are talking!" and separates from it and goes its own way. In everyday life, the mind considers the heart stupid, and the heart considers the mind cruel. Thus, the separation is made wider. Religions thus were created to command the mind to bring it back to work with the heart. However, the existence of too many religions also makes the mind confused. The mind cannot know, "Which one of these religions is my true partner?"

Friend, if you have achieved enough, you will know that the essence of the religious teachings is the return to the universal heart energy; beyond that, there is no secret. However, religious promotion with all its different literature, philosophies and ideologies is still the product of someone's mind. It confuses people who are trying to learn spiritual achievement. However, the differences between the religions, literatures, philosophies and ideologies are not in conflict; they can be treated merely as variety. Each one is just like a style of cooking. There are lots of differences in cuisine. People can enjoy them all or enjoy what is most original. What commitment should be established? It is all simply like food with slightly different flavors.

Spiritual achievement is deeply related to spiritual reality. Nature has two spheres: physical and spiritual. Physical knowledge is now very much developed, because everybody recognizes the usefulness of science. As to spiritual knowledge, the habitual psychology of the authorities of religious convention makes people wonder if spiritual knowledge is useful, because the religions have gone too far from natural truth.

It is universal heart energy which directs the discovery of and the truth of universal spiritual reality. So, for someone who is looking for religious consolation and support, it falls on the emotional level, where nothing is related with the truth. Look at your pure heart, and you may find the truth. Your heart contains all the truth, be it expressed by any name or any way. When you reach the heart, you have reached the total truth of a religion and what all religions can express.

All of us are the offspring of nature. We need to learn from nature. We need to learn and discover how universal spirituality can support our development, internal spiritual integration and spiritual harmony.

In this book, I am pointing out that no one who lives in the world should neglect extending his heart energy to his own life, family, friends and the world. At the same time, because life still has the two different levels of mind and heart, we must not let one project too far to one side without the corresponding association of the other. We need to extend our heart and mind in a unified, healthy direction. Fundamentally, all achievement is the progress of our spiritual condition. Once our spiritual condition has improved, our mind will be clearer than an unachieved mind.

So the cooperation of your right and left brain is precious. The unity of your mind and heart is also precious. At a level higher than your right and left brain, there is no more right and left; there is only your precious spiritual nature, which embraces the enhanced soul. We work on the soul so that we may achieve the Inner Light to shine upon our internals and externals. Thank you for using this book.

Your spiritual friend,

Ni, Hua Ching
November 10, 1989

Chapter 1

Introduction

I

The material in this book, *Internal Growth Through Tao*, is taken from the interactions of daily modern life. The modern conception of life is more superficial in the levels of material goods, emotions, lovemaking, moneymaking and psychological satisfaction than it was in ancient times when people lived quite simply and naturally. Most people have achieved or completed something on those levels. However, they do not touch the much more subtle sphere of life. They also do not know what is the right spiritual direction, or what is a good direction for each individual life.

Basically, in working on this book, I have put together material related to these subjects. All of my teaching concerns internal growth, but this book in particular is almost a conclusion of my intellectual service to spiritual students.

Concerning external achievement, we already understand material achievement, emotional fantasy and psychological satisfaction. They are three components that organize or comprise the path of external growth. I do not belittle those achievements. Surely, if a person does not have external growth, how can he have internal growth? But those things, the external matters of life, are customarily the teaching of general educational institutions: schools, parents and society.

As a spiritual teacher, I teach internal growth, which is different from material achievement, emotional expansion and psychological consolation. Whatever your mind is made of, or whatever kind of achievement has satisfied you, that is external growth. Yet, above the levels of body and mind, there is still the spiritual life or internal level. The spiritual life connects with your mind, emotions and what type of life you lead, but the focus is different. This type of learning makes your internal essence grow above the pressure or stress of external achievement.

Without internal growth, a person's external achievement is like a false flower that the soul of this person is unable to really enjoy. Anyone who does things for the sake of appearance will find that the fruits of his efforts only have the quality of looking good. But once a person really attains internal growth, he builds a real strength in worldly life. Thus, inwardly a person has spiritual achievement and externally he has worldly accomplishment to make the balance of a good life. This is the model of a good life.

In this book, I talk about the nurturing of spiritual sensitivity. Why? When a person pursues external achievement, sometimes there is too much cruelty. Sometimes there is too much contamination of the soul. Both cause spiritual insensitivity. Not everyone is aware of the reality of the universal spiritual subtle influence or even of one's own internal spiritual condition. Without this awareness, without internal growth, external pursuit of material achievement becomes negative work that undermines a person's good life.

In this book I teach the more subtle, much deeper sphere of the reality of life that is above the shallow sphere of external achievement. I also show the lack of growth and confusion caused by some spiritual teachings of an external approach. Then I guide you in the direction that helps a person develop spiritually by growing internally. This book is very special for those people who have some vision and ask themselves: "What am I doing in the world? I am busy with this and busy with that, participating in all the parties and in all kinds of excitement which pull my life in so many different directions. What is myself?" This book is a service for people who engage in achievement in external life, and, at the same time, would like to attain internal growth.

Once your internal growth is attained, I believe you will become much wiser and choose the level of external achievement that will satisfy you. You will project your life energy in the right direction and you will project your life energy effectively, without causing wasted energy and struggle. This describes how this book can serve you.

In our life, emotional matters are sometimes very costly. We spend the "money" of our life energy, symbolically, to support our psychological expense. In other words, we use our life energy to pay our psychological expenses instead of investing it in internal growth. But what is the difference between our psychological life and our internal growth? Our psychological life is made up of what we hear from astrologers, psychologists and religions, and from the attitudes of the people around us. Internal growth is developing the most useful and helpful qualities or features of a human personality. Internal growth is not expressed as maturity or sophistication in handling the world; that is still worldly, not spiritual. Internal growth is nurturing, spiritual self-guarding and enhancing one's positive spirit of life to unlimited development.

Your soul, your spiritual energy, is connected to a deeper, more subtle sphere. A careful reader can find the answers, direction and cultivation in this book to look for that growth. This book is especially helpful when complemented by the study of my other books. It is for those individuals who would cultivate internal growth.

II

Generally speaking, I am a teacher of Tao. My Western friends call what I teach Taoism. The concentrated Taoist teaching is not to allow one's natural being to become sickened by worldly experience, spiritually, nor be confused by human cultural creations, conceptually. It is important always to maintain one's organic condition of life on all three levels of body, mind and spirit, poised in a position of natural life. These few lines basically describe the essence of the teaching of Taoism.

We cannot reject the creations, confusion, correct achievements and mistakes we have experienced in these past three thousand years. The Taoist people, who are mostly interested in the natural life being, are certainly aware that we cannot go back in time to the society of 3,000 years ago. Practically speaking, we all live in the same society and expose ourselves to all kinds of social maneuvers, cultural activities and wars. From an agriculturally centered society, we have moved to an industrially centered society. Now the commercial culture is in the lead.

So, how can a person grow, from existing in an unnatural environment to receiving the teaching of natural life? Once people's lives begin the drastic change to modern times, what is the new approach or new direction of developing the soul? There are hundreds of spiritual customs and big and small religions. People want to know which of them, or if any of them, can guide one to the truth. However, almost all of those human religious cultures and external structures describe the understanding of the ancient leaders' spiritual attainment. They expressed insufficient spiritual development instead of total spiritual development. Their basic mistake was that the leaders did not understand that spiritual development is the internal development within their external being. Once something is over-externalized, it cannot be directly related to the source, which is the original and organic spiritual nature of human life. The followers tied the spiritual practice to the religion or religious founder instead of to the true spiritual source. Religion can never accurately describe the spiritual reality of human life and nature. Thus, achievement in spiritual learning comes from the direct path, the internal path of spiritual teaching.

What is the direct path, in contrast to the indirect path? The indirect path is the literary nature of all general religions. They do not directly tell you or teach you the spiritual truth, which they have not yet reached, but instead assertively offer some incorrect and spiritually prejudiced social programs with the purpose of attracting believers and supporters. They dominate the believers' minds and attempt to decide one's thoughts, life activity, behavior and spiritual communication. It is not a fault that they establish an indirect teaching by using metaphors to describe the spiritual reality of humans. However it is a fault to define the metaphors as truth and insist that the believers absolutely accept the definitions.

Generally, religions can be experienced as having one kind of activity. In one kind of religion, there is a god or many gods. What is god? Or what are the gods? Who is god, or who are the gods? These separate gods are described through the use of metaphors or stories. This is the indirect way of spiritual teaching.

In the direct path of teaching, the teaching is truthful. Metaphors are used in teaching truth, but they are accepted as metaphors. It is not the same as the indirect way to teach. Direct teaching guides a person's spiritual energy to come back to the spiritual center of the natural being of each individual. God is not an external path. God is your main soul.

Therefore, two kinds of teaching are experienced. One, the indirect way, has a great production of literature passed down from the ancient teachers to be taught as the spiritual reality of each individual. Metaphors are taught as truth. Whatever people are told sounds like something external to them; it sounds like something else, somewhere else. However, they are not really talking about spiritual reality. The way they talk about it reflects the stage of growth of the teacher. In whatever way, they are not really talking about spiritual reality, the way they talk about it reflects the stage of growth of the teacher. So now, you can see that the indirect way is the roundabout way of teaching through metaphors and literature.

The direct way has nothing to do with external establishment or indirect teaching. However, in teaching the direct way, an instructor still needs to quote the indirect teaching. This is one of the features of direct teaching.

The teaching of Tao is an internal path instead of an external one. Please understand: indirect teaching is external religious teaching; thus, direct teaching must be internal teaching. External teaching stresses the structure of external things, such as temples or churches, or the differences in customs and rituals of religious performers. The ceremony of religious performers, the language or terminology and the institution of thoughts and conceptions all become part of the external establishment which teaches a person to fit a mold that someone else has designed for himself. The result is that spiritual truth appears to exist outside of him. People use different language, different layouts of thoughts and different types of literature to describe the same one reality which is individual spiritual reality. Some students are still somewhat confused as to why Taoist rituals are any more the "truth" or are "a better way" than any other religious, conceptual, relative ritual. Some serve your deep understanding to build a thoroughfare for the mind in achieving spiritual transcendence while other practices serve the effective life which was developed from the above kind of mind.

The teaching of Taoism values the natural life being. It is the foundation from which one derives growth. The teaching of Tao is not one of those rigid teachings that mold you into some kind of robot. The teaching of Taoism is direct teaching instead of indirect teaching. It is internal teaching instead of external teaching. But frequently, to achieve the purpose of the teaching, it is necessary to use the established external teachings, because those also express stages of achievement of the human mind. It is helpful to use those established external or indirect teachings to demonstrate the direct path to people who are used to external religions.

The direct, or internal, truth expresses simplicity. Yet it seems that the simple truth is so condensed, so tight, so high on the steep cliff of a mountaintop while the students are at the bottom of the ravine. Therefore, in teaching Tao, the existing material of external and indirect teaching is frequently used to teach the direct path at the same time as the internal path.

Taoism is a teaching which holds the essence of all religions; it becomes a transreligion. By that, do I mean it is transportable and intercommunicable among all the religions? On some levels yes, and on some levels, no. For example, the teaching of Christianity has its simple essence. The teaching of Islam has its own simple essence. The teaching of Buddhism also has an essential teaching. You might think that Taoism teaches the essence of all those teachings. If that were the case, Taoism would be simply an organization of data or a compilation of writings from different sources. The ambition would be to take every good thing to put into a big pie. Here we see what distinguishes the original teaching of Tao from the folk tradition: the tradition of the Union of Tao and Man continues as the pure teaching of Tao. The Chinese folk Taoists teach a mixture of many religions. Often sects combine teachings from many sources. They virtually no longer present the simple essence of the teaching of Tao. In other words, folk Taoism, with its different sects and occult practices, is a combination of external religions. It is like the dish from the kitchen of a Cantonese restaurant called Chop Suey. The words "chop suey" mean mixture or combination. Folk Taoism is not the pure teaching of Tao nor have those people reached the Tao. The simple or essential Taoist way of teaching is not something stirred up together without spiritual discernment.

Taoism is the direct path; it is an internal path, an essential path. It means to hold the essence of all religions. It does encompass the essence of all external teaching. No popular level of religion has reached the spiritual essence at all; they mostly attempt an external description. The individual frame or structure of each one holds the essence of that particular teaching, but they do not present the essence of universal truth. When you describe Taoism as a teaching of the spiritual essence of all religion, you must have a clear understanding: it did not take the essence from any of the religions. The teaching is the spiritual essence of universal nature directly, but it utilizes the method of comparison. Through describing an external religion or teaching in a given situation, we wish to carry the main teaching or main thought to the student.

For many years, I stood on a platform to teach in public. When I read over the transcript of my lectures afterwards, it appeared that I frequently talked about external religions. Please, my teaching must not be misunderstood. Each religion presents something. Religion works with a certain function of the nature of mind and a certain stage of people's mind. In teaching Taoism, we do not deny the existence of other religions. A religion is a rough emotional or psychological expression of people and society in general that has been expressed or concentrated and transformed into a religion or system of belief.

I do not deny the symptoms of the problems of religion. So I discuss the problems to suggest a cure. We are aiming to offer a remedy for the shortcoming of the psychological lack of development of people. The remedy offered by Taoists is the best existing material to awaken people's deep spiritual nature. Human society has already paid a big price for its own undevelopment. Why not take the lesson from it? When the teaching of the universal spiritual essence is given, examples from all different religions can easily be gathered.

It is important to know that in the process of human growth no stage can be replaced by another one until it has been finished or worked through. The time span that a person spends in each stage, though, can be shortened by accepting and learning from a relevant teaching.

As a Chinese proverb says, "Each of the sellers of watermelons proclaims that his watermelon is the best." It seems easy for someone to say, "My watermelons are sweeter than the watermelons of another seller." However, I am not in competition to sell watermelons. I am a watermelon eater. I know the truth of all the watermelons that I have tasted. The knowledge of different spiritual teaching connects with each individual as a much deeper influence than the eating of watermelons. Practically, I teach a student to nurture good spirit in himself. Taoism is spiritually nutritious. It nurtures by guiding all the students to return from the external religious confusion to their own spiritual center for healthy growth. I hope that it is clear what kind of teaching I do.

Sometimes I meet a new person and am introduced as a teacher of Tao. People feel interested. Since I came to the West, I have written many books in order to respond to all the questions and to help straighten out people's unclear understanding of Tao and of what I teach. However, it is possible that many friends or students still do not know what I am doing, or what the main structure or nature of the teaching of Tao is. For these reasons, I have taken this opportunity to talk about the nature of the teaching that I do, and to express to you what you can learn from this book.

The direct teaching and the internal teaching is the direction of my own cultivation, and it is the direction of my worldly service. All my work is moving in this same one direction.

Chapter 2

Tao Serves You Spiritually

Q: Master Ni, we are students of Tao. It is not easy for us to grasp. What is Tao in everyday application? Would you kindly tell us your own experience? How did you learn it?

Master Ni: Tao is realized in everyday life. When I was a teenager, I gathered a group of young children in my neighborhood as my followers. They liked to sit there listening to what I said because I had learned the tongue of my father and teachers. I was proud of that. In doing so, however, I often neglected my duty as a family member. I lived upstairs by myself, and the rest of the family lived downstairs. At meal time, I made the whole family wait for me to come down because I was in meditation, studying the holy books and scripts, and I continued doing that.

One day, I really upset my mother because it was a cold day, and the food she had prepared was best eaten warm. I always made my family eat cold food because of my tardiness. My mother thought it was not proper for me to do that, so she decided to give me a lesson. She said to me, "You think quoting lofty phrases from the books is Tao. You keep meditating upstairs in your own room and call it Tao. You think reading those books will make you the friend of the sages. You think it is Tao, but it is not Tao. It is your personal enjoyment. You know, when I was young, I was similar, having fanatic thoughts about Tao, and I also behaved like you. I thought that what was everyday and mundane was really secular and unholy. But then I really was enlightened to know what Tao is, so I married your father and gave birth to you four children. Since then, I understand that to give birth to children is Tao. To raise them is Tao. To feed them is Tao. To change their diapers is Tao. To make clothes is Tao. Everything in life that you do seriously and find meaning in, is Tao. Anything beyond the necessary duty, contribution and positive attitude toward life is not Tao.

"If I did not think it was Tao, why give birth to you? Why do I keep the daily routine of washing, cutting, cooking and serving the vegetables and the other food, waiting for all of you to come to eat? I do it because I think that is earnest life. At no time do I cheat myself. So I make a connection with heaven. I am self-respecting. I credit what I am doing. I think my life is righteous, I do not take advantage of anybody. I am not dependent upon anybody: I do my part, do my share, and by living so, I do not need to consider whether I have Tao or need to attain Tao or anything else. You think that just reading and gathering people to listen to you is Tao. That is not practicing Tao."

This is what my mother taught me. So if a person truly understands Tao, he does not insist on the formality. He can teach Tao and apply Tao in any occasion in his daily work and life.

The fish lives in water, but one day the fish says, "I need to attain Tao. I need to move to the mountain." This is a bad choice. He cannot live on the mountain. He leaves the Tao to look for some self expansion. That is what you do. The great path, the great principle of spiritual cultivation is to maintain your balance, maintain your good concentration in everyday life, like holding a bowl of water and walking in the dark. If you do not balance yourself well, if you do not have a strong sense of morality, if you hit anything, you will spill the water. This is the value of spiritual cultivation: enlightening yourself to see through your own darkness, to maintain your balance. This is the first principle a person needs to achieve. Then we can talk about the other high achievements and development.

Q: Master Ni, we would appreciate knowing the nature of learning how Tao differs from other religious beliefs; would you kindly tell us?

Master Ni: To learn Tao is the pursuit of spiritual sobriety or soberness. I use the word sobriety. The people of general religion are looking for numbness of their spirit or awakening of their spirit; they are drunk. They are looking for the ecstacy of emotion. They do not need the truth. "Just come to talk to me - make me feel happy. Right or wrong, give me a story." The religions make them feel loved, needed, wanted, helped, recognized and respected. To learn Tao, you do not need that. You need to attain your spiritual independence. You do not become muddy drunk, either conceptually or spiritually. What do I mean by muddy drunk? A person of good sense has a certain shape or form and can talk about it or communicate. But a person who is muddy drunk or intoxicated is like a basin of mud with a lot of water. Even with a stick, he cannot take one bit of mud out of it. There is no way to communicate with such people, because they are drunk. They love it. They may be ready to die for this kind of quasi-religious society or religious teaching.

To learn Tao is to learn spiritual sobriety. Sometimes we use the words clarity or purity. This is the sobriety that is different from the muddy drunkenness of general religious faith. If you understand this point, this is what I think would be helpful for us to learn. If you choose to say: "No, I am weak, I feel pain, I would like something to make me numb. I want to feel ecstacy from intoxication," that is different. That is not the way to learn Tao, it is not the way to learn about spirit.

I choose the way of spiritual sobriety. People may think it is the hard way. However, if it is the way, why is it hard? Most people cannot do it. Yes, all people could start by taking a little help from the sages' religious teaching. But that is not the final destination. The final destination is to attain sobriety and independence of spirit. This is the highest goal, because it is difficult for a person to decide what is high and what is low.

You must understand, my hard work is necessary because the world is so confused. Among the confusion, I need to do something to help those people who are looking for sobriety of mind and spirit. Any person who attains clarity can immediately check out the falsity of any religion which totally depends on lies, or perhaps not so much on lies as on relative understanding and different levels of relative concepts. Unfortunately, most people are not knowledgeable, so they become confused. They are not looking for the ultimate truth. But they try to combine all the dishes, all good teachings from different traditions if possible. Then what they gather, good teaching, still does not reach the ultimate truth and the higher teaching. It seems that this is what people do who are looking for the truth but do not know where to look. But they cannot learn truth unless they directly learn Tao. After learning Tao clearly and firmly, they can be helped by reviewing all other teachings. Then they shall surely know that they have already reached a high spot to look down to where they were, and they shall discover they have attained the strong vision which can disperse the smoky unclarity of religious literature and go beyond the lower emotional texture with no more bondage.

Religious freedom is necessary, but my spiritual work is to clarify the confusion so that people can find the true source, the true help, the spiritual truth which, being light, can help all people. I cannot consider myself above anybody, but this is the way I learned. This is my family tradition and spiritual reputation. So if there is anything against sobriety, I do not know how it can be called truthful. When a person is sober, he may tell me, "Master Ni, tomorrow I am going to do this for you." If he is drunk and says the same thing, which words do I accept? Those of the person who is sober or drunk? How can you tell? What real difference does it make? It is a different point on the path. A wise person would take the words from the time when the person is sober.

A sober person driving a car is trusted. When he is drunk and asks me to sit in his car, I will not do it. Which car would you like to sit in? The one with the driver who is muddy drunk or sober?

There are two kinds of spiritual paths: in one kind, the driver is sober and clear about what he is doing; in the other, the driver is drunk. We do not support drunkenness, we support sobriety. This is the total purpose of our work.

My own writing can be unattractive to some people because I use stories only when they are necessary. I teach the truth by the most direct way in order to save time and avoid misguidance.

Q: Master Ni, you enlighten people by using all opportunities. Would you give your own insight of how people can learn about spirituality?

Master Ni: People have their own psychology. People have their own emotions. At times, people need external support, especially when they are in a psychological predicament. Therefore, if a person reaches for any religion to help himself or herself for the purpose of psychological support, we do not think it is a bad thing to do. It is proper for everybody to have some psychological support from a good source at any time. However, often when a person resorts to religion, it means he has already lost the basic foundation from the general world and cannot find any more support. Maybe the psychological balance is not there, and therefore he has grown a kind of internal insufficiency.

Sometimes I call religion a crutch. In the world, there are sick people. They may not even be aware of their sickness; however, they reach for a crutch unconsciously. I always have sympathy for those people who need a psychological crutch. I teach recovery. I teach health. I recommend that healthy people learn Tao. This is what I learned from the training of Tao: Tao is the individual's own spiritual unity. It is more necessary than anything else. It is the fundamental achievement everyone needs.   Once you have reached spiritual unity, there is no disharmony or conflict inside and no disharmony or conflict outside any more. You are perfect in health. When unity is lost, the next step down is where a dualistic situation is established. Duality is yin and yang. A dualistic situation is typified by two sides of polarity: a feeling of separation or of differences. Harmonization of two elements is what one would best be looking for. However, harmonization does not eliminate duality.

When an individual looks for help from an external source, the relationship of guest and host is established. In the situation of the relative sphere, any two things in duality have the relationship of guest and host. To use other words, I am describing the relationship of subject and object.

For example, each individual is a subject or host. Any external source to which an individual looks for help is the object or guest. Thus, a host can look for help from a guest. Let us take the following four situations as examples to illustrate the possible relationships between host and guest:

1) We live in the world. Each of us is a guest in the world but each individual thinks he himself is a host. Considering oneself as the host is a function of mind.

When a host is strong and a guest is weaker than the host, the guest needs help from the host. For example, a student is helped by a teacher or a worker is helped by a boss to do a job. This relationship means the host is stronger and more helpful than the guest. Sometimes the roles are reversed. The function of a worker is to help the boss do his job, although a boss often has to first train the helper. Here, it appears that the external is stronger than the internal. The guest is stronger than the host.

2) Conversely, a person looks for religious support because he, as the host, is weak. Religion is something people consider joining, learning from and participating in because they need help. This relationship means the host is weak and the guest is stronger.

However, in the instance of a weak host and strong guest, a certain situation sometimes occurs. When the guest is stronger than the host, it is an open opportunity for the guest to either help or to eat up the host in an dominating situation. The guest might be dominant over the host. In the case of religion, this is where the person is dominated or taken over by the religious guidance.

So, after examining the above two situations, we might ask the following: Who can be helped? In neither of these can a person be helped. The one type of person who is capable of being helped is the person who does not lose the vision that whatever external belief helps him as the host, it is still a guest - in other words, the help is separate from him, not a part of him. Because his life substance needs help, the host goes to the guest for help. Though the host needs help from the guest, balance between them is still needed. If such a balance is lost, it does not mean help, it means being eaten up. This is a personal psychological matter. In most but not all situations, the objective or ideal standard is that the host and guest are equal. It is through the effort of the host that poise is attained.

3) In any situation where there is an opportunity to establish a relationship between host and guest, the two sides

are always looking for balance. Mutual help between the host and guest does not occur when the guest tries to squeeze, grasp, drain or push the host. Nor does mutual help occur when the host tries to force, deceive or kill the guest.

So there are three situations which describe potential relationships between the guest and host. The fourth situation is not a real relationship at all. It is a type of emotional vanity or luxury on both sides; because it is emotional, there is no true relationship, only fantasy.

Let me give an illustration. This may not be easily understood or seen as being a guest/host relationship. It is an illustration of a person's fondness, such as having great enjoyment or desire for a particular thing. In 1949, the Chinese government withdrew from the mainland to Taiwan. Some young military officers who came from the mainland stayed in the southern part of the island in a base for new training. Those young people stayed in the training center during the week, with little opportunity for recreation or diversion; thus it was very boring. Since each person's psychology, emotions and ambitions are different, different kinds of entertainment are required to restore psychological balance. So on vacation or holidays, some of them went to the neighboring countryside or neighboring city to spend their time, and that was enough for them. Others needed more.

At that time, on the island of Taiwan the best entertainment was a Peking opera show starring a famous woman actress. The show played each week in the city of Taipei, which is located on the far north end of the island. To restore their psychological balance, during their weekend off, some of those trainers needed to go as far away as Taipei to watch that opera. Not only did some of them take the trouble to travel all the way to the other side of the island to see the actress, but some went to greater extremes. They needed to do much more to regain their balance.

As you know, when a person goes to the opera, sitting in the front row is more expensive. It requires early reservations, and the tickets are much more costly. Those who chose the front row also had a long travel time. In those days, going from south to north was a nine to twelve-hour ride sitting in an old train which was very crowded and noisy.

The young men who needed to watch that opera in order to restore their psychological balance only had one short weekend in which to do so. So they went to all the trouble of making the reservations and tolerating the twelve-hour train ride to Taipei. Then they were satisfied, and came back with the psychological strength to face another five or six-day ordeal of boring military training.

But even those people who went to the north to watch the opera were different from each other. Some bought only a regular seat and were satisfied. Some needed to spend most of their salary to buy an expensive seat and sit in front. Some went even further, needing to buy the most expensive flower basket to give to the actress. It is really incredible the amount of warmth that can come from an admirer. Yet some of the officers did even more. In the southern part of Taiwan, there is a city called Ping Tung where big watermelons are produced. It is hard to carry a big watermelon while sitting in a crowded train. Yet some young gentlemen did this traveling the whole way to Taipei to watch the play and give the watermelon to the actress. In such a case, the balance of host and guest does not exist. However, the host thinks he has fun. Such behavior totally comes out of one side's willingness.

In this fourth situation, there is no real relationship between host or guest; there is, however, personal wishful thinking or imbalance on the part of the host. For example, the opera actress in Taipei created a great attraction to all the young officers. The fascination and enchantment was surely produced by the actress, but mostly it was produced by those people who enjoyed watching her. The responsibility for their troubles was not hers. Quite often such a time-consuming and exhausting trip to the opera meant failure during the next examinations and a delay in arriving back to the base meant receiving a certain punishment. The woman was not at fault. None of the people who had trouble tried to use her as an excuse. But whatever punishment or failure they received, they accepted with a kind of happy willingness; they were willing to sacrifice themselves just to watch the sweet face of the actress. They were all ready, brave soldiers, to die for that kind of "high morality far away from the real battle-field." They had that kind of willingness.

This example parallels what happens in religion and art. There are sometimes external things which will fascinate, enchant or bewitch people. Religions are similar to such an opera show in that they are entertaining. If anyone puts a lot of energy into something, especially on the emotional level, the good feeling or joy is returned. In religious feeling, if a person has enough maturity to understand that the feeling is spiritual, he knows that there is no real gain from it, but if he likes to do it, he does it.

But as you know, religions have a special promise that a person shall go to heaven; psychologically, this is a great attraction to a person and makes him believe wholeheartedly. But once the person comes to his end or death, it all fades away because faith is a conceptual structure and conceptual structures belong to the mind. He still comes back to the plain soul. Even if his mind was fascinated, enchanted or bewitched, at the point of death, the conceptual structure all fades away. So all his psychological hope is emptied.

The idea behind teaching Tao to others is not to absorb or pull the learners' strength and energy away from their balanced lives. A person who learns Tao learns to put away his worries and dissolve the vision of polarity or duality in the world; this is returning the individual soul to the individual. In the world's arena, the hunt for money, fame or power, and the attraction of art, religion and sex all pull an individual out and away from himself. The teaching of Tao makes a person wake up again; he slows down while still enjoying everything, and all without losing the balance between the position of guest and host. The learning of Tao is putting the sense back in the individual.

As I described, the amount of entertainment each individual needs is different. Life itself needs entertainment. Good religions are also entertaining; a good preacher is also a good actor. People can enjoy what they like. My teaching is not to show you what has monetary value. I am teaching spiritual balance in all games of life, including the game of believing in a religion. You cannot be crazy or lose your head for your enthusiasm; if you do so, then what is your spiritual growth? I am saying you can be somewhat crazy, but do not lose your head in all the game playing.

I have mentioned that religious belief is the promotion of the spirit of drunkenness. If a person is not drunk with it, he does not enjoy it. On the other hand, the learning of Tao is the promotion of the spirit of sobriety. It teaches a person to keep awake, alert and aware while he is drunk with what he likes. This is art. This is spiritual achievement. You might be interested in attaining it.

There are people who utilize all kinds of psychological attraction with religious coatings to take advantage of others, making them lose money, fall or experience misfortune. It is nobody's fault. It is a person's own preconditioning that makes him easy prey of the world.

So now you can see that the teaching of Tao promotes sobriety and awakening. It is artful practice and application. It is not like other religious teachings. If you are really wholly awakened, you will not like the game of life any more. You may learn the way of Buddha, which was totally to abandon worldly life, not allowing even a small desire to remain, to withdraw from his social position, and to be a holy beggar for one meal each day among the villagers. However, to be a student of Tao, the standard of art is higher. When you know the game of life is bitter, you must not befriend the bitterness of life. When you know the game of life is sweet, you cannot become attached to the sweetness. So, the way of the Taoist plays the game of life with an awakening mind in drunkenness. At the same time he maintains the drunk feeling, he is fully awake and aware of his responsibility. This type of awakened drunkenness, or wisdom maintained in foolishness, is termed the elixir or the wine of immortality. This is what the immortals enjoy. It is the secret of becoming immortal.

Taoist teaching encourages people to enjoy their lives and to have all kinds of fun or trouble; however, both during and after having fun or trouble, they still remain themselves as sensible and balanced in their real life. Other religions suggest hating life. They can pull you away from real life.

Let us say that a person buys some alcohol and drinks until he becomes drunk. That is basically all that happens. Once a person has a religious belief, however, that is not all.

He has drunkenness in his religion; he does not only enjoy it
by himself, he pulls his own family and friends into it, always
saying, "You don't know the truth. You don't know how good
this is." This causes great disharmony, because he is not
happy when other people do not listen to him. Some people
don't agree, but think that one person's drunkenness from
alcohol really affects his family and pulls it down if it happens
repeatedly. I might say that those two types of drunkenness
are the same instead of different in their effect.

It is interesting to see a person already sitting drunk at
a table at the roadside tavern. He watches people so busy in
their lives and declares that all these people are all drunk or
foolish. He never knows he is the one who is drunk and
foolish, but he always accuses other people of being drunk or
foolish. Similarly, those religious followers, once they come
to a situation of fervor, when they open their eyes, they feel
the guilt of the world. They think that people are pathetic.
They never know that they themselves are the ones who need
to receive sympathy. Whatever a person sees in someone else
is only a projection of his own reality. He does not know that
he has already lost his balance. Any kind of unbalanced
drunkenness causes aggressive attitudes. That kind of
drunkenness should not be encouraged.

In the next section, I would like to talk about what the
teaching of Tao actually is. Especially in China, there are so
many small sects, groups and leaders who use the words of
Tao to attract people. It works because people do not have
time to directly learn or achieve Tao. They use those words
to attract people easily. So now I would like to talk about
what is Tao.

Please, do not wonder when I say that Tao is not an
existence and that Tao is non-existence. Any established
thing, whether it is on the material, conceptual or emotional
level of faith, is a thing. All things are in one same category.
They are not Tao. The source of those things, before anything
is established, before any name is given and before any
concept can be described, whatever is still within that origin
is non-existence. That is Tao. Tao does not have any
evidence of its existence, its substance and its identifying
characteristics; it is not up or down, not left or right, not blue

or red, not anything. It is Tao. There is no way to pursue or search for Tao, because to search is to move further away from Tao. Tao is where you are before you start to search. Can Tao be caught? Tao can be caught, but not by language or concepts, not by either movement or non-movement; Tao is here and there and everywhere. So the general religious approach by which people look for Tao is a deviation from Tao. Some people say, "I have already gained the Tao"; that means they have lost the Tao.

People do not understand the reality of Tao, because Tao at that level is difficult to teach. The secondary or tertiary religious approaches that attempt to teach Tao in China are confusing. You, my friends, may ask me, "Master Ni, if Tao is non-existence, then what are you doing? Your books have existence." I am teaching Tao. Though Tao is not existence, we can use the existing things to show the non-formed Tao. We do not do it by being limited to one single object; we use all of them to show the non-formed Tao.

For example, we are walking through the trees, and the moon is shining brightly in the sky. You are new life. You do not know anything. I discover the moon. You might not see the moon yet, so you ask, "Where is the moon?" My finger pointing, I say, "Here is the moon." Students watch my finger and think, "Oh, Master Ni's finger is the moon." They do not realize that the moon is not my finger, the moon is where I am pointing. When I converse with a new student or new teacher, he does not look at the truth, but he takes the description of the truth as the truth. That is the main limitation of his mentality.

Tao is fascinating to me. Tao is what I enjoy a great lot. Learning Tao is to learn the simple essence. Other learning might only be the dregs. Dregs cannot make people grow; they only burden people. When we learn from either the ancient or the modern wise ones, we especially need to know whether we are learning the essence or the dregs. The conventional religions are the cultural dregs. They cannot make people grow unless the people are already wise. Growth depends on yourself: to know how to take essence from the dregs and how to take essence from the essence. This is the principle of Taoist learning which was established 2,500 years

ago by Lao Tzu. To take essence is a power; it is the source
of all power, new, converged, constructive power. It is the
source of progress. It is not merely a belief and it cannot turn
out to be merely a doctrine of general religion. So the
teaching of a doctrine, whatever it might say, is only talking.
Where a person points, is only a dancing finger. You do not
see what he is pointing at unless you get rid of the obstruction of the image of the finger; just from that direction will you
see the moon. This level is harder in teaching, so there is a
second level. What we call Tao is the mother of the universe,
or the universal mother. It does not still need to be a
concept.

But if a person starts with concepts, he may never stop.
Let us simplify our thoughts about Tao, and you will see how
the problem of religion began. Let us say that a person calls
the nature of the universe father or mother, because it is the
source of all lives. Once there is more and more remote
conceptual creation, he is farther away from the origin of the
universe. For example, his students will say, "oh, there is a
universal mother; let's worship the universal mother." So
then the worship of the mother is established. Then, they
begin to wonder, why should it be the mother of the universe
instead of the father of the universe? And then, what does
the universal mother look like? To deal with these questions,
a wise one finally invented the symbol of tai chi; the top side
is black and the lower side is white, or vice versa. He used
this to tell the students that this was the mother or father of
the universe. Is the symbol of tai chi really the mother or
father of the universe? It is a diagram demonstrating the
ultimate truth, the integration of two forces, the masculine
and the feminine. From that, everything is brought about and
continues to do so.

But then the students began to wonder, in which heaven
does the mother or the original one of the universe live? Well,
there are three big heavens. Each heaven has twelve heavens. To sum up, there are thirty-six heavens; that is what
was taught and was recorded in the ancient books too. So, in
which heaven does the mother of the universe live? Their
questions will continue. To give a conceptual answer to that
question, because each heaven is part of the universe, all

divisions of the heavens are born from the mother of the universe. A person can have them all by reaching the universal mother or the original one. The mother of the universe is not any one of those heavens, because she is the mother of all. To use more simple language, she is the subtle origin.

So people establish the beliefs of the mother of the universe, but they never know where she is because they do not live in Heaven. She lives in all heavens at the same time. And also, she is not only external; she is also internal. Practically, each individual life, after being born into the world and establishing its individuality, is the mother of the universe. You can see that life is so creative. In each moment a person cannot stop his thinking. Each thought is a projection and gives birth to something. A person continues to issue energy from inside outwardly, never stopping. Are you not a small model of the mother of the universe? You are. Once you cease to issue energy, once you cease the capability of giving birth to new things, you cease to be the mother of the universe and wait for the natural recycling by the great mother.

Here, I would like to interrupt that thought. When I was a student, I was not attracted by any philosophical discussion or mythology. I was fascinated by the thirty-six heavens. Each has its specific name and function, and each has deities or spiritual inhabitants. Later, I was amazed that the ancient teachers did not have powerful telescopes as modern people have. They did not have spacecraft, artificial satellites, the theory of relativity or complicated mathematics and calculations. However, they viewed the universe, the galaxies and the heavenly bodies in a way that was so close to modern astronomy on some levels. They were particularly detailed in their descriptions of the different heavenly energies. So I concluded, there must have been someone among them who had experienced ascending to those Heavens. In those records, they described the stones from stars pouring and shooting like the rain in a storm in some area of outer space. If they had not experienced it, how did they know? It is marvelous. These things were what I enjoyed learning and exploring. I was not looking for something to believe. I was looking for something that would expand my tiny life being. Ancient Taoists scarcely talked about saving the soul. Some talked about ascending to Heaven. They knew which heaven should be visited first and so forth and recorded it with great detail. Because people of different backgrounds have different intent, I do not promote that to you.

The technique of exuviation in Taoist teaching is only a small secret. This relates to the soft dead body and the effect of touching the mystical point. Even so, what is the preparation and the next step of the exuviation? Some people have not learned it and are satisfied by having the knowledge of this small technique. This is sort of like the story in the book of Chuang Tzu, in which the King of the River was proud of its fullness of water before seeing the ocean.

Religiously, people worship the products of the creative energy, while Taoists worship the productive or reproductive energy of the universe or nature. Without this reproductive energy of nature, people could not continue. That is the typical description of Tao. Generally, when people hear about this, they say "Oh, great, reproductive energy," and think that this means to go have sex. That, however, is not what we are describing. Though we nurture the great reproductivity of the universe, in individual practice we always look back to the reproductive origin whence we come. That is where we receive our new life opportunity. That is what makes the universe eternal and gives the possibility of eternal life. Because we are a small model of the universe, we also have our reproductivity; do you think that this means giving birth to children? No, reproductive in this sense does not mean sexually. We are talking about productivity in our life: cells and energy. This natural operation is not something that you and I can manage. It is not the mind that manages it. It is nature that operates it; we just enjoy the ride. We appreciate the riding. The learning of Tao brings us a great appreciation of riding the converged natural substance of life, more than external beliefs that make a person become a martyr for what he believes. We greatly appreciate riding the natural energy; this is far greater than riding any of our conceptual creations.

The devotional activity of following external belief is actually against universal internal truth.

Each person needs to reach his deep understanding and needs to reach a spiritual connection with his internal reproductivity. Each person needs appreciation of life. First, calm down your mind to discard your worry and ambition. Then, let the center of reproductivity keep functioning beautifully with no interference from your mind, including externally imposed beliefs.

I would like to talk further about how a person's external beliefs can affect his life. Once when I was living in Taiwan, I witnessed two men of about the same age, in their early thirties. Both had a liver problem caused by emotion. For the first one, my instruction was simple: to move to the countryside and live a simple life, where he could breathe good air. At the beginning he needed some help from herbal teas. Because his liver problem was a whole life problem, he needed to change his life. He was never to touch alcohol and never be angry or frustrated about what he could not achieve; then he would be a happy person and his problem would be solved.

The second person had the same type of liver problem, but unfortunately this person joined a church. This church encouraged people to pray madly, saying that only praying could cure a person's trouble. It is true that in some cases, prayer can help, but in other cases similar to the first man's, peace and order are necessary for improvement. This is not to say that we do not encourage a person to release emotion; just that it is better to disperse the emotion. The difference is that if a person talks about emotion, then he will create even more emotion. It can escalate. Prayer is talking, so if a person prays about emotion, his emotion will only increase. This was the opposite of what the young man needed, so his case was a failure and he died.

Of these two persons, one was a simple sort. The other was more literary and emotional. So the less emotional person survived. The more emotional one did not survive the swollen liver disease.

Humans come to different stages. They have a chance to contact all different levels of teachings. Some will bring benefit to a person, but others will bring trouble; it all depends on what the person takes up. This is similar to choosing a car or one's companion, occupation and so forth. Peaceful living and strong belief in God have different functions when they are applied to different situations.

The basic thing I have offered is my pure service. You can enjoy only reading about it and talking about it, or you can continue to make it an important principle in your lifetime practice. It totally depends on the situation of your own growth. It is a way of teaching Tao. Each person grows in his own way. You can grow your way. Nobody can really teach another person unless the person knows his growth occurs by absorbing, rejecting, filtering and digesting. Pearls are not appreciated by swine, only by beauties. Only when a person has some spiritual understanding is he open to something light and good, healthy, durable and worthy.

Q: We would like to know if there is any special understanding that can be used to distinguish a good teaching from a confused one? We need something that will help us decide quickly what we are going to learn. We need to know what teaching or knowledge is worth pursuing without wasting our energy in studying something that is useless or misleading.

Master Ni: First of all, in being a good student, do not worry too much about wasting energy. The reason is this: at the beginning you might believe that something is not beneficial, but if you are a person of positive energy, you always can learn something there. Sometimes you can gain much from an unbeneficial situation. One important principle a Taoist teacher can give to his students in their practical life is to have courage and clarity of mind to try new things or face many kinds of life situations. Similarly, a person cannot always decide to refuse the many unpleasant, unhappy or even harmful situations existing in one's life. The good outcome of any situation still depends on you; you can turn an unbeneficial situation around to be beneficial. If there is any secret of life, if there is any one game a Taoist likes to play in applying his life energy, it is not to work out his own created situation, but a situation given to him.

Once a student related her own experience to me. She referred to this principle as "the hidden gift." Any time this person had to accept unpleasant, boring or less glamorous jobs, less than ideal living or sleeping situations, poor companionship or material insufficiency, and so on, she stayed with the situation and applied herself to it while looking for its hidden gift, which is the benefit in a difficulty. It was often some kind of learning about herself that made her understand life, herself or others better. Sometimes it was acquiring proficiency or skill in order to make unpleasant jobs quite pleasant and fun to do. Sometimes it was material benefit, an unexpected opportunity or a new friendship. Almost always there was also spiritual learning. Sometimes it was learning that she did not need to accept certain attitudes or kinds of treatment by other people any longer. It all depended on the situation that life gave to her in that moment. But there was always a benefit for her, as long as she stayed long enough and positively applied herself to the task. After she learned to do well with it, she would receive the benefit or learning. Difficulties lost their power over her because she knew there would always be a pleasant surprise hidden somewhere. I feel good about her achievement; thus, I quote her experience here.

Because you ask me to give you a simple principle to distinguish clear, good teaching from confusion, surely you already know the goal of spiritual learning. The test of a teaching's benefit is to attain natural spiritual unity within or not. If that spiritual unity can be achieved truthfully, not by a false story, then you will know that it is the supportive, useful and helpful learning of the individual self, the group of true people and the entire society.

If you stay at the level of following the religions, you will not reach spiritual unity. It cannot be attained at the level of religion because there are many religious differences, until you learn Tao. Tao is the uniqueness of spirituality itself. One must have the need to learn all different religions and their varied expressions in order to attain the truth underlying all of them. One can directly learn Tao. Tao is the essential spirituality that expresses itself uniquely and is different from all other ways.

In many different situations, I have spoken on how to distinguish between Tao and religions. The principles have also been previously discussed. But in this specific situation, I will again point out the distinction between the two stages: 1) Pre-Heaven or Above-Heaven and 2) After-Heaven.

The ultimate truth exists only in the Pre-Heaven stage. If any possible confusion or a segmented part of truth is held as truth, it exists in the stage of After-Heaven. For example, although Taoism is internal spiritual growth, in one stage, the sages taught us to worship the God of Ears, the God of Eyes, the God of Nostrils, the God of Tongue, the God of Hands, the God of Organs, the God of Feet, and so forth, in order to guide people's attention back to their own natural life. It is natural exposition from the deep sphere of nature, which we call spirit or nature. So we have equipped ourselves with ears, eyes, nostrils, a tongue, organs, hands, a body and feet. All these things are not what you order or design for yourself. They are natural gifts. By recognizing such a big fact, this teaching guides people to come back to their life, so that they are not pulled away by external attractions or over-exalt external and material pursuits.

In the next stage, the teaching was different from the first stage. Now the sages taught the people to worship the ability to see, the ability to hear, the ability to touch, do, live, walk and so forth instead of the God of Ears, God of Eyes, and so on. They changed because in teaching the God of Ears and Eyes, etc., the students might think that those different gods exist. So they changed to talking about abilities. They pointed out that any ability such as seeing or hearing is associated with the entire being and also with the seeing and the being seen, the hearing and the being heard, etc. If there is no such interrelation, the ability to see, hear, taste, smell, do or walk cannot be established. Any single expression of capability is related to the wholeness of truth. This is the second stage of Taoist teaching.

Earlier, we mentioned that the ultimate truth is only in the stage of Pre-Heaven or Above-Heaven. First there is the subtle origin; once there is a division into the After-Heaven stage, the functions of hearing, seeing, smelling, tasting, distinction by feeling and so forth arise. Ability is what is behind seeing, hearing, smelling, tasting, touching, feeling, doing, walking and so forth. Ability is one; the functions are many. When ability is applied to a specific function, the specific function shows itself, but it is not disassociated from ability. Ability stays behind the specific function.

So at this time, maybe you have a better understanding when we say that Tao means the potency of nature. Tao is the ability of nature to produce. What is produced? We consider that all of the products are in the stage of After-Heaven. Potency or ability, whether before or after being exhibited, is in the stage of Pre-Heaven or the subtle origin. However, it is also true that the stages of Pre-Heaven and After-Heaven are not absolutely separable. They exist together. There must be something to issue the functions or ability to see, hear, taste and so forth, once expressed, in order to achieve the purpose of the function. The ability must work through a form such as the eyes or ears to achieve the purpose or function of seeing or hearing. However, in all the situations, the subject and the object are established at the same time. No one side is the only truth that can be conveyed. So ability, form and function are expressed as wholeness.

An advanced student who learns Tao knows that the product, for example, the product of hearing, which is communication, is not what is to be worshipped; it is the mother of the product, which is the ability or potency behind what is produced and is what should be caught by attention. The discussion of ability is limited in its scope, because ability has further distinctions such as the issuing ability and the receiving ability. But those are divisions; the single essence should be caught, thus we are learning Tao. To reach the Tao is to reach the whole. There is no other name that can replace Tao and have the uniqueness and the wholeness of Tao.

To move to the third stage of understanding in Taoist development is to know further that there is truly no distinction or difference between ability and function. Any function is the expression of ability. Ability is the source of function. When there is confusion, it should not be seen as confusion, but decide immediately on what level a thing belongs, whether it is a product or it is original potency. I mean, if a person is confused about something, he can often find his way out of the confusion by determining if he is dealing with an ability or a function. To decide a thing by different levels and stage of nature, when we talk about the original, pre-Heaven stage, we are talking about ability or Tao.

The profundity that a Taoist can reach, when he touches a leaf from a tree, is this: he sees the branches, trunk and roots of the tree, and also sees the earth where this tree was alive. I am not talking about literal vision. To have this type of vision is a matter of growth. Most people might hold the leaf, but they cannot attain the whole truth of nature. Their vision is limited by their limited experience of life. This is why the Taoists say that the wholeness of truth can be presented by a blade of grass. But what you experience depends on the depth of your understanding. If you cut off all connection from a leaf, holding the leaf as the wholeness of final truth, you would be missing seeing the wholeness of truth. If from one grain of sand you can see the vast desert or the vast shore of the ocean, then you have attained growth and reached great profundity. One's vision is not a matter of differences, it is a matter of growth or maturity.

There is no trouble with the spiritual differences among religions if a person has reached the profundity of natural spirituality. By this I mean, the differences between the expressions of spirituality as exemplified by the different religions are not important to one of profound natural spirituality. For example, in the fine arts, different tools, styles and materials result in varied artistic expressions. Different training also makes the artistic expression unique and interesting. Those fine arts bring forth differences, but they do not bring an argument. They bring about different appreciation.

Spiritual teaching on the level of after-Heaven is the same thing as fine arts. The different spiritual expressions are all unique and interesting. All of them can be appreciated without the need to argue about them.

I would like to give another example. Many people know from my books or lectures that on many occasions I discuss T'ai Chi Movement. We have many friends who are fascinated with T'ai Chi Movement. However, they do not know that many masters who are achieved in T'ai Chi Movement are also able to do Shao Lin, Hsing Ye, Ba Gua, and many kinds of weapons as well as T'ai Chi Movement. T'ai Chi Movement represents a broad approach that many teachers especially need to exalt for people, so they use it. In their life, what is most valuable is the ability to do T'ai Chi, to do Shao Lin and other different kinds of martial arts. The ability to do the movement is the most valuable thing in each life. It is not the different style or exercise that makes something valuable or not. The typical believer, however, will pick up the frame, form or style and think he has gotten something. To the person who achieves absolute freedom, there is no frame. This is one example of how people need to see that precise forms are not what life is about.

To learn spiritually is to attain the mellowness, ripeness, maturity, sweetness and skillfulness, of the mind, spirit and body. No formality should make you caged. In the process of learning something, anything positive, a person can reach spiritual growth. Becoming refined is to reach mellowness, sweetness and skillfulness, the smooth application of your own mind and spirit. Once you know the goal, you will know the teaching material that is right for you. A different style or school is only one subject. It is one stepping stone; it is not the goal. The trouble that all religious followers have is making the ladder the goal. They perceive the road to be the destination. They are stuck there singing Hallelujah.

In my opening talk, I mentioned that people of different understandings or stages often have difficulty communicating. Each individual is an individual world, and communication cannot always go smoothly between individuals. Especially in the case where people who have reached maturity are facing those who have not, they find that they are in two different worlds of communication. However, between spiritual friends or among those of the same level of understanding, there is no longer a solid wall of separation; communication can go through. When an achieved Taoist and an achieved student meet, why are they are so happy? They do not need to rely on discussion, speech or language. Each individual's movements, postures, expressions, speech or silence are all communication. Each of them understands the other quite well. Not only do they understand, but they have also learned the correct response to most situations. All the truth of the profound universe can simply be expressed by a sigh, some laughter, a sneeze or even a fun noise made by an achieved one.

The difference between the teaching of Tao and general religion is that to teach Tao is to teach the achievement of the ancient developed ones and to use it appropriately. To teach a religion is to establish and promote an individual and rigidly follow his teaching. The purpose of spiritual learning cannot be forgotten. It is to reach the essence. Once you know where to go, you are not bothered by the differences in the styles of learning of the different schools or religious expressions. Things can be discussed; it is from discussion that we learn. What is important is that you keep yourself on a path of learning internally and externally, and looking for more depth and understanding. I myself do not think I know much; only this much have I reached, as you have now.

Now I would like to present two short stories. Once a person decided to buy a new pair of shoes, so he did his homework. He made his measurements precisely, because precision was what the person respected. It is truly important, we all agree on this. He lived in a rural place, where there was an open-air market only once a month some distance away. On market day, he rode all the way on his donkey to find a shoe vendor. As soon as he arrived, suddenly he realized that he did not bring the measurements he had made. Then he got back on his donkey and rode the whole way home to look for the precisely described measurements. Now that he had the measurements, he returned to the market for his shoes, whipping the donkey to make it keep going. Unfortunately, it was now afternoon and the market was over.

The reason he could not buy his shoes was because he did not have the precise measurement. He did not realize that he carried the real things, his feet, with him all the time; he only remembered that what is on paper is important.

The second story is that many times I have asked some of my students to drive me places. All my students are good intellectuals; they are developed, highly educated from college or other institutions of learning, and are good at reading maps. The purpose of going to school is to attain knowledge. A person who has been to college must be knowledgeable, more so than anybody on the road. However, so many times, when we came to a new place, in the right spot, I would sit in the car as my student driver examined his map, over and over again. Unfortunately, he kept going around in circles, because he could not figure out where he was. What he could remember was what was on the map, although he knew where to go once he found that out. Much easier, however, would be to stop and ask a gas station attendant to verify the location or the directions.

Beloved friends, doubtlessly, God is precision and God is accuracy. But they are not in the descriptions on paper, they are as near as your own good life.

Now let us go a little deeper and talk about a question that is crucial to all religions. It is the topic of the soul.

All religious teaching is declared to be a means to save your soul. Its purpose is to cure the world's spiritual problem. In order to accomplish such a task, one must definitely know what is the shape and nature of the human soul. What does it look like, does it have any special nature? How does it need to be saved? How does it fall? If a person wishes to save the soul of all the people in the world or even just his own, he must first have true knowledge about the soul. The knowledge of the soul that you have now, did you hear it from somebody? Or do you have proof, yourself, that you have a soul?

It is my understanding that one's spiritual nature in heaven sometimes can be called heavenly destiny or heavenly fate. The spiritual nature is each individual's true self. Saving the soul is making the individual know the value of living a worldly life. Whatever he does, if he meets the Tao, or our teaching, it is to meet heavenly destiny or the heavenly commandments. If a person is able to do that, it means his soul is saved.

From my understanding, I am talking about universal spiritual nature. Spiritual nature is the same in everyone, everything and the individual source. A soul might be collected, saved or restored to its original purity and wholeness, but that is not spiritual nature. I believe, if I understand you correctly, we might consider that spiritual nature and the enlightened individual soul are not different things. But that is not true, because the soul is blocked by the undeveloped mind.

Spiritual nature is good and consists of beauty, holiness and completeness. Individual reasons such as time, society, inheritance and other influences make each individual soul appear differently, just like the nature of all the different types of vegetation. For example, in water and on dry land, vegetation will express or grow differently. That is because of the influence of the environment.

Everybody's original spiritual nature is the same. There is no possibility of it having any environmental influence before a person is born. Once the individual's soul takes the form of life, then the life in its different environment will express a difference because of the environmental influence.

This is the first thing I would like us to recognize: that the original spiritual nature and the individual soul are not different. There is a difference between everyone's original spiritual nature and individual souls after worldly experience.

The spiritual nature is the soul. The soul is spiritual nature. The teaching of Tao promotes spiritual independence. However, without saving the soul, there can be no spiritual independence.

It seems to me that if a person truly understands spiritual nature, he can achieve spiritual independence without the need to be saved. The action of having somebody come to "save one's soul" is secondary, external religious teaching. Spiritual independence ceases to exist when a person leans or depends on external religious teaching. In other words, true "soul saving" is done by an individual for himself or herself, not by one individual for another. The teaching of Tao is not like religious teaching because we do not come to save you. If you learn Tao, you learn to work on yourself. This is why we provide self-study materials rather than attending any kind of weekly services. We wish you to become strong by your own efforts, because then it is your own achievement and it is real. Other people need religious help; that is also okay, but to become independent without using a religious teaching is one form of true achievement.

Some people do not know they have a soul or that their spiritual nature exists forever. Mostly they are only aware of what they see with their physical eyes, which is that all people must someday die and leave the world; their body will be left to rot. However, although the body is destructible and returns to the dirt and mud, each person has a spiritual nature that endures. The way the spiritual nature is formed, and what happens to it at the moment of physical death, depends upon what a person believes. In other words, if a person changes his faith, he changes the way his spiritual nature is formed.

So everyone's body dies and the spiritual nature endures, is good and is not harmed. In other words, living in a body is like wearing clothes or like being in a house. Why then, do the religions promote saving the soul? If the soul never dies, then what must be saved? That is a valid question for examination by spiritual students. Basically, what it means is that a person's pure, uncontaminated soul or spirit needs to be protected from the traps of worldly life. It is in the traps of seeking material wealth, physical pleasures and social glory that the original positive spirit of a person becomes muddy. Most souls have experienced worldly life, and so they have to clean up their souls a bit. Some would say that it is because through sixty thousand years of reincarnation the souls of all people have become contaminated by worldly life, and they have to be saved or cleaned of the contamination. This is why many people, in their lifetimes, took so much trouble to look for a teacher to save their soul. Because they have new reincarnation, they need the teaching of high sages. What I say is from the real sages who became the immortals.

There are different levels and aspects of spiritual teaching. Sages taught different aspects of spirituality according to what they knew best. Many sages' teachings were only about general life and how to regulate the mind. So many taught this because "saving" or decontaminating one's soul is accomplished in living an upright, balanced life. Do you see the point? Because living an upright, balanced life is the means for purifying or maintaining one's original spiritual nature, there is no need of separately teaching saving the soul apart from an earnest, honest life.

Some sages' teachings were only about general life and how to regulate the mind. The soul was saved by living in an honorable way. Thus, there was no need of separately teaching the saving of souls. In religious activity, they also thought that spiritual offerings to the spiritual world would help. They thought their wishes would be fulfilled. Some sages withdrew from general religious teaching, because they were seeking truth. We understand that saving the soul is not accomplished through religious ritual, but instead through each individual's cultivation of his spirit. Practicing rituals does not save a person's soul. Only through an individual's practical and truthful self-cultivation can a soul be saved. But on the practical sphere, what general religion offers is an attraction, something that serves a person psychologically. It does not address the spiritual level.

Saving the soul is a common subject of the religious levels of teaching. It is a way to organize rituals and beliefs. No one really sees the true spiritual effect on the soul unless people do hypnosis, channeling or other spiritual phenomena. It takes truthful spiritual cultivation and achievement of the individual self. No superficial ritual, practice or doctrine will reach the soul. Those things are just like any other worldly experience.

External religious activities may make a friendly emotional connection. Truthfully, they have no value in the search for truth. There is no improvement of anyone's human soul.

An important improvement of an achieving soul, one that is no longer on the worldly level, is that it is not partial in supporting any particular religious teaching. Such a person does not accept any sermons from anyone. After having experienced the world games, that person truly understands how and what the low sphere of the human mind wishes to manipulate.

Saving the soul is a process of undoing the obstacles we have gathered through our life experiences. So the unnatural being is the obstacle to a wholesome life being, the well-being of life. The well-being of life is the well-being of the soul. As other religions have discussed, because there is so-called sin or original sin, the practical way to save a soul is to improve ourselves by undoing the poison we have gathered.

Through a belief system, surely, psychologically you feel delivered, and you feel your soul is saved, but it is not saved. Your soul remains in the same stage and never changes a little bit, unless you deeply improve something in the structure of how you construct your life being. The main soul itself and the gathering energy of the soul are partners. Both compose the soul. Thus, just affecting one level of the soul by bringing about a joyful feeling to it, as in some religious practices, does not improve the healthy condition of the soul. It is still not complete. It is just like going to a poor country and seeing a beggar. If you give him a check, that might make him feel good, but it does not benefit the reality of his life. He cannot cash the check. Similarly, the religious spiritual promise from the faith to save the soul makes the person feel good. However, it cannot be cashed. Belief is one thing, and the believer is another thing. Belief is external, it is not internal. Internal is from the true spiritual nature, directly manifested. If the spiritual nature is sick, the manifestation is sick.

Therefore, all good spiritual work contributes to the health of the soul. The soul cannot be separated from your entire being. Your entire being cannot be without a soul. Therefore, the soul can be treated by correct spiritual education, so that you can engage in your spiritual cultivation. Without correct spiritual education, only applying one's believing energy, one only becomes more sick, not more healthy.

All religions present a stage of growth of human spirit. All religions have made their contribution in a certain stage of human life. If you are looking for spiritual progress, if you are looking for spiritual growth, you can never carry your cradle or use a diaper your whole lifetime. You must stand up. You must use what you already know. If you learn something more, keep open to something you have not known. Our soul needs new light, new fresh experiences and maturation. Otherwise, the soul, the spiritual life will become stiffened and dried.

The principle we follow is that first we watch and take care of the fundamentals of our own life. After doing that, then we develop ourselves more. But if a person has not taken care of the fundamentals to live a constructive life, for example, then attempting to save other people's souls is not practical.

As I have learned, we live a practical, earnest life and we do what we can do in the scope of our walk of life. It is enough to make a contribution of our own life to the lives of our associates and the lives of some people of the world. We consider that it is a constructive life. We do not need to do anything separate from our rightful way of life like trying to save souls.

Chapter 3

Taoist Folk Religions

A Discussion with some Chinese and American Students about Chinese Folk Taoism.

Q: Master Ni, as we know, there are a number of Taoist teachings active in the United States. Sometimes it is confusing because they teach different things. Some people have been around here locally who say that they are members of a religion called "Tien Tao" or "I Guan Tao." They say that their religion is a combination of all religions, and use teachings from all different religions to give their message. I went to one of their meetings and found it to be quite different from anything I had seen or heard before. Could you please comment on this?

Master Ni: It is not my interest to comment on different religions, for several reasons. First, religions are both positive and negative; which aspect a person receives depends on his ability to perceive truth and his relative standpoint to the religion. Second, religions have different levels and people are at different levels of growth, too. Third, if a person is conceptually tied to something, he must usually figure it out for himself if it is not correct.

As I have mentioned in many places in my books, in the Tradition of Tao, we would like for people to learn the natural truth that is above the teaching of any religion. It is true that there are several different "new religions" which take their teaching from a combination of many different religions. "Tien Tao" or "I Guan Tao" is one of them.

Trying to combine the doctrines of various religions is taking a mental approach to learning truth. Until the natural truth is reached, however, the mental concepts are often confused in the minds of the followers. Because people are in contact with so many different teachings, yet never deeply understand them, they become confused. It is always necessary to help straighten the wrong impressions that people get from misguided information or misguided teachings. So let us discuss any questions you might have about what you have experienced or heard.

Q: I have looked in a dictionary and found the group listed there as "originally an outlawed quasi-religious secret society in China." Being outlawed is the reason that this group has recently changed its name from I Guan Tao to "Tien Tao", which means "Heavenly Tao." Could you start by talking a little bit about the background of "Tien Tao"? Is "Tien Tao" from China?

Master Ni: This particular movement of this religion came to be known publicly at the beginning of Dr. Sun Yat Sen's new republic of China in 1912 around 80 years ago, after the Ching Dynasty fell. The original goal of this group was to abolish the Ching Dynasty and to restore the Ming Dynasty. So when the Ching Dynasty was finished, their activity still continued.

There are books that talk about the historical background of the teaching called "Tien Tao" which is now called "I Guan Tao." It says that it began about seven hundred years ago, when China was ruled by the irresponsible grandson of Genghis Kahn. He neglected his responsibilities of governing and enjoyed the practice of full-hearted sexual tantras; this created an opportunity for all kinds of revolution among the people.

At that time, one revolutionary leader used a story given in a book to attract people to become his followers. It was a false Buddhist book which tells people that Sakyamuni is the Buddha of the past and that the future Buddha will be Maitreya. It is said that when he is born into the world, the lotus flower will blossom. Mr. Han Shang Tung and his son were the leaders of the revolution. The father made the book claim that the lotus flower blossomed when his son was born and therefore he was the Maitreya. People often believe such things on the level of the literal wording. As we know, many young boys and girls are born in the time that the lotus flowers bloom, but only one father said that this young man was a new-born Buddha Maitreya who came to deliver the world and help the people help their souls. So they organized a religion with a special mantra, ritual and teaching. They attracted many people who were dissatisfied and resented the ruler, the grandson of Genghis Kahn. By these means, Han Shang Tung started a revolution.

At the same time, there was another spiritual group in China called Ming Chiao, which means the religion of brightness. Its parent spiritual group was Manichaeism, whose origin was in Syria. It was initiated by a man called Mani (or Manichaeus or Manes) who lived from A.D. 216-274 and was based on the spiritual customs of the Middle East combined with some teachings of Taoism. So the group called Ming Chiao and the group of the so-called Maitreya, which was called White Lotus, began to compete for the power of the throne. The people of Ming Chiao, whose leader was Chu Yuan Tsang, won the competition for the throne. Then the group called White Lotus led by the false messiah, Maitreya, scattered, became active underground and continued to look for ways to seek power. Many smaller rebellions started by this group in later times were defeated.

This struggle between the false Maitreya's group and the people in power continued endlessly. The only purpose of White Lotus' existence was to gain ruling power. After the Ming Dynasty (1368-1643 A.D.) was conquered by the Ching Dynasty (1640-1911 A.D.), the White Lotus group changed their slogan to the restoration of the Ming Dynasty and abolition of the Ching Dynasty. Then, after the establishment of the new Republic of China in 1912, it became one of the Chinese folk religions. Later during the Sino-Japanese War, the "Maitreya's" group was used by the Japanese and also by the nationalist government to hide spies; their type of religious activity was hidden deep within the villages and countryside, and at that time, police stations were not as thickly deployed as today. After the Sino-Japanese war (the Second World War), Communism started. The Communists did not continue to use them for spy activity because they had already attained power. Subsequently, this quasi-religious society withdrew all of its activity because the new Communist government did not allow it. Only a traditional, natural society has enough freedom for people to do whatever they like, so the White Lotus withdrew to Taiwan.

They then started to use the name I Guan Tao, which means United Tao. They teach a mixture of Buddhism and Confucianism, and use the folk Taoism skill of magic writing as their main tool. Magic writing is the ability of a spirit to give messages to the human world by using a person in a trance to write messages. The critical point is that I Guan Tao has no genuine spiritual purpose at this time. This religion has a strong ambition to group people for political purposes. Through its 700 years of history, this quasi-religious society has grouped several times and gathered energy to start rebellions in China.

This religion utilizes the names of all sages in the magic writing, but not the sages' real teaching. Although I Guan Tao started around seventy years ago, with the same Tien Tao slogan under a different name, it refers to sages who already have an image of authority in the minds of people and society. It claims that its tradition started with Fu Shi, then went to the Yellow Emperor, Lao Tzu, Confucius, Menfucius, Sakyamuni, then to the sixth patriarch of Zen Buddhism, Hui Neng. This made it popular among the people.

I would like to say that it is possible that the Chinese spiritual tradition started from Fu Shi, then went to Shen Nung, Lao Tzu, Confucius and Menfucius. But how could it be passed to Sakyamuni directly, who was born in Nepal, in the south side of the Himalayas? At that time, transportation and communication were impossible. Then how could Sakyamuni's teaching come back from Nepal to China to inspire the sixth patriarch, Hui Neng? It is historically unlikely that the teaching could have been transferred.

According to I Guan Tao, the lineage of the teaching went from Confucius to Sakyamuni Buddha. However, Confucius lived and died earlier than Sakyamuni. How can a person pass his truth to another person who was born after he died, perhaps about a hundred years earlier? The time sequence does not even slightly show the possibility. The proof of this is given by new Buddhist scholars.

At that time, there was a great distance between the cultural center of China, which was in the northern area around the Yellow River, and the Indian culture, which was centered far south of the Himalayas, a distance that most people could not overcome. Also, there were no maps, no knowledge of geography and no similarity between the Mandarin and Hindi languages. Thus, people could not communicate. Passing spiritual teaching is mostly by oral communication. It seems highly unlikely that these two people could have passed their knowledge to each other.

Also the teaching presented by I Guan Tao or "Tien Tao", called the big vehicle of Buddhism, was a later development of that religion which occurred 500-700 years after the death of Sakyamuni.

It is, however, possible that there was influence passed between the spiritual teachings of the north and south rather than any kind of exact passing of the lineage.

The initiators of I Guan Tao or "Tien Tao" continue by saying that Sakyamuni's teaching was passed from Menfucius. From reading the teachings of Menfucius, Confucius and Sakyamuni, I observed that each writing by itself clearly covers a totally different subject and has a totally different nature, although Sakyamuni did not directly write any books. Many scholars researched and discovered that the true origin of Zen Buddhism was Chuang Tzu, not an Indian master. The supposed Indian origin was a reflection of the fanatic belief of the Chinese people who adopted the northern Buddhism.

It is clear that the leaders of I Guan Tao or "Tien Tao" use a kind of image to support people's faith. They announced that heaven authorized them to do the teaching, and they hint at being the sovereigns of China. They said this 700 years ago, 70 years ago, and the present group in the United States says it now, hinting that they are spiritual sovereigns authorized by Heaven. I do not know how they can receive heavenly authorization; Heaven is an individual experience.

A long time ago, the leader of this group put together this so-called tradition, but he did not have any real knowledge of Buddhism. His followers are always confused about Hinduism and what is truly Buddha's teaching. They put all the religions together just to take advantage of the religious structure. Buddha never said he was going to save the world. He never had that ambition at all. However it is a fact that this religious group uses that slogan to gather people under its fellowship and control. We do not know the motivation behind it. Because people feel lonely, they need a tool to reach out socially and help them accomplish their individual interest. The purpose of the leader is to group people, and take advantage of those who do not have time to study all the truth. They use the words "to attain Tao," as meaning to join them or to learn from them.

It is my understanding that the leaders of the original group were not really high scholars. They were not people who had deeply studied the history and become true leaders. They were always people of half knowledge. The followers were intellectually weak and undeveloped people who did not study the reality. This is also true of the level of followers of any religion who do not have the time or interest to reach the high levels. If a student or follower is truly interested in gaining an understanding of spiritual or religious teaching, I recommend that he or she look to the source, such as what Buddha actually wrote, rather than relying solely on information such as what comes through magic writing. Magic writing is a phenomenon that occurs when a man is put in a trance and a ghost comes to give the message through him. He moves an instrument to write in sand.

It was another fact that the leaders of I Guan Tao used the grouping method to influence the vote in Taiwan. They forced the government to legalize their quasi-religious society as a formed religion from a secret movement among folk people. Every day they use magic writing; they teach the words in the names of sages. They even use words that are not from sages. They use the new theories to teach people. They never give up until they think they have influenced people enough.

Historically, when enough people gained confidence in the group, the leader started a revolution by announcing, "let's choose the teacher to be the new king." So then riots started and cities were attacked. Many times the followers of this group were caught and beheaded. The believers sacrificed their good but ignorant lives for the ambitions of the leaders.

To promote this quasi-religious society, usually a team of one teacher and one magic writer is sent to a new place. The magic writer is usually a young man, woman or child who is manipulated by an older teacher. All teaching is given through magic writing or false books to which the names of sages are given as authors. This group usually does not stay in a formal temple; they rent a house in a neighborhood and invite people to join. Usually they do not go to the intellectually developed community, they go to farmers or people who are unable to read. Their technique of gathering people is to attract people who have spiritual curiosity or concern about their ancestors.

Many people participate in activities of low spiritual stature; they do not know when they are just being fooled. They are then encouraged to promote these activities to their friends.

This is how the group called I Guan Tao, which is now "Tien Tao," achieved such fast growth. The original leaders were people of political and revolutionary motivation. It is their habitual behavior that the spiritual practice is totally an organized scheme to group people as a mob. The new members know nothing about the group's origin.

If all the world's religions started at that level, it would be discouraging to join any spiritual groups or religions. Fortunately, true and false can be distinguished by a person's development.

Q: So you are saying that this is not an objective spiritual teaching, but a political group disguised as a religion.

Master Ni: Spiritually, if a teacher is really achieved, it does not matter if he borrows somebody's authority or name; it is important that what he teaches is right. But the skill of this society is to borrow the name but not the original teaching of these sages. They are used and taught to people after being twisted. Even if the motivation is to help people, especially to help people's souls, they affect people's minds. If the teaching is not upright, then people become prejudicial in their lives.

Being a spiritual teacher, if one chooses to do so, a person must give strong moral reflection to the worldly problem. Then one responds uprightly. There are so many uneducated or undeveloped people who cannot see their way clearly in the world, and they can be so easily fooled in their own attempt to find out what is good or true in life. Or their life condition or level of understanding places them in a situation where that is all that is available to them. This is why I so strongly wish that all people learn by themselves; so that they can avoid their own innocent involvement in something more powerful than themselves.

Many people are good people and do what they can in their lives to help others. But unfortunately, not all are like that. The same is true of religion; some are good and do give some help to the world, but others do not meet that standard.

Let me go back. All religious teachings have their book of origin. The teaching of Buddhism has the Buddhist canon, translated from India in the Sanskrit or Pali language to some Chinese writing. The Taoist tradition has the Taoist canon. New books can surely be written, but any writer needs to be responsible and put his personal name on it. In some religious teachings, the leaders do not put their names on their books; they just say, Buddha says this, and make lots of new books. This Buddha, that Buddha; they are false books because the author uses the name of Buddha instead of his own name.

Some religions have an aggressive approach in gathering their followers. Whoever comes to them, they say "We are helping your soul," and use all kinds of communication. They say, this is the only truth. They utilize the word Tao. A truthful teacher does not need to attract people aggressively and pull them in. All he needs to do is express what he teaches; saying, "this is the truth I present." People either choose it or they do not.

Q: So this group had different names. So if I study about different religions, I might come across the same teaching under a different name, right?

Master Ni: In the historical record, any time this religion made trouble, it changed to a new name. It has been called the Ba Gua (the diagram of eight hexagrams in eight directions) religion and the Lung Hua (Dragon Flower) religion, and many other names.

I understand that language is changeable; in fact, it is often desirable to use different wording to teach old concepts to awaken the minds of people. However, the name of this religious group changed each time the reputation of the society was troubled.

This group restarted seventy years ago to continue using the slogan of fighting the Manchurian Ching Dynasty and restoring the Ming Dynasty of the Han people. At that time they used "I Guan Tao." Let me tell you where this conception of I Guan Tao comes from. It is from Confucius; he says that for correct human behavior, there are two main practices. One is loyalty and one is forgiveness. One should be consistent with them. I Guan's purpose was not the uniting of the religions. He did not say, I am oneness with three or five different religions. His way was persistence, which means he did not change his virtue at any time. It means to stay faithful to your mind, your knowledge, whoever you contact and what you are doing, and be forgiving. This not changeable. "I am always persistent to realize that virtue is an important part and expression of my life being," is what Confucius teaches.

Although the name I Guan Tao was adopted, the original teaching is totally misunderstood and misapplied. Their group does not understand the virtue of persistence. At the beginning it was called the White Lotus religion, then after some trouble was caused, they changed the name to many others. Later they changed it to I Guan Tao, United Religions, and most recently, to "Tien Tao" or Heavenly Tao after its legalization. However, the truth of the origin and function of the religious society is the same, no matter what the name.

Q: Can you tell us something about the religious practices of this group?

Master Ni: The essential practice of Ming Chiao was "eat vegetables and conquer satan." I Guan Tao is to become a vegetarian only. They think that if a person eats any animal life they will need to pay a debt for it in the next life, and that only by eating vegetables can they ascend to Heaven. They do, however, include eating eggs of chickens and ducks. The nickname of this religion in Taiwan is the religion of duck eggs. Some other religions similarly treat vegetarianism as the only approach to being holy. I agree that vegetables can be good for one's blood because vegetables give healthy help. But I do not think that eating vegetables is the only way to help a person spiritually. Spiritual development is mind development, and it is true that the mind is very connected with one's food and diet. But one's diet is not the only sign or signature of a spiritual person. Some people eat vegetables and think that they are holy. It is considerably a healthy diet and a spiritual diet, but not a symbol of spiritual achievement. I believe it is okay to adopt a diet that includes non-vegetable food, that is a balanced diet, but I discourage killing animals or birds.

"Tien Tao" followers consider eating eggs as a part of vegetable eating. Are not eggs life? So the leaders of the quasi-religious society mostly die of high blood pressure because they accumulate such high cholesterol from eating too many eggs; they even put the eggs in wine to assist their sexual energy. In my understanding, I do not see how eating eggs can be the same as vegetarianism. This is why I call it false, not truthful, discipline.

They say that there is a reason for the chicken eggs: it is a heavenly gift. They noted that when Sakyamuni meditated in the forest, one morning he felt hungry and he received milk from a shepherdess. His drinking milk caused all his followers to depart from him, not because of the woman; but because he was not supposed to eat anything except at noon. They were disappointed that he did not keep his discipline of Jainism's ascetic practices. The leaders of Tien Tao told the followers Buddha could accept milk, so they can eat eggs.

It is clear that all good food is a heavenly gift. Eggs, vegetables, meat, fruit, grains; all are given. For a healthy life, each individual needs to learn how to eat according to his own needs and physical condition, in order to support the body, the body to support the mind, and the mind to support the spirit.

This society says, eat eggs and you can ascend to Heaven. They also charge ten dollars as a starting "fee of merit" to ascend to Heaven. I believe this is not correct understanding; if ten dollars could send you to Heaven, I would buy a ticket for all you without sitting through the class. In that case, I shall feel sorry for all the sages who worked so hard to achieve spiritual quality in order to make one small inch of progress.

They think their teaching of going to Heaven is based on the three main teachings of Confucius, Lao Tzu and Buddha. But in the teaching of those sages, no mention was made of ascending to Heaven or anything about the three stages of total destruction to unbelievers. They never said anything like that, or about the time of the green sun, red sun and white sun. It is totally a peculiar theory twisted from the study of the *I Ching*.

Whatever they say has no connection with real worldly life. It only talks about a stage of ritual, and even the descriptions of the rituals are not accurate.

Some religions use a special posture when they see each other to show that they belong to the same group. To them, it was the signal of the black society that they belonged to. This is not necessarily true of most people who mistakenly join them. Those people are victims and are being used.

They used the story of a carved stone which was discovered due to erosion on the bank of the Yellow River as proof that their tradition is supported by Heaven. I read several years ago that at the time the Japanese invaded China, people were scared by the Japanese soldier's cruelty; they thought it was doomsday for China. In fact, this tradition used the same scheme as the leader, the bandit Sung Jahn, who carved the stone, buried it there, and discovered it to assure his leadership. The leader of this group used the same trick to proclaim "doomsday is here, come to me and I will save your soul."

I mentioned earlier that it is immorality that I am against. Actually, people themselves are often innocent of the results of their actions. When darkness comes to society, it is not always the people who are bad. They are only misguided by a stronger energy than themselves. This occurs not only in religion, but other areas of human life. Let us take the example of communism. Some communists might have had a good heart and a good motivation toward the cause of improving society, but their method and thoughts caused them to lose balance. They only brought more trouble with their fanatic motivation.

How can a person know what is true and what is not true? Both are taught. It is all teaching. How can you decide? As we know, history repeats itself, politically, socially, religiously, etc. One can study the *I Ching* to learn more about how all things cycle.

I would like to talk further about what undeveloped spiritual teachers do. I hope that it will help keep some of you from falling into trouble. When an irresponsible teacher likes a woman, he will say, "the sages said it is nice to have a holy person to sleep with." If he does not like the woman, the teacher will say, "we must be celibate." They all quote the truth and say that something is for spiritual health or physical health; they do not tell you the real purpose. They only have an emotional, desirous purpose, and make use of the sages' names to support it. In any religion, there are always some black sheep. People can, however, get true information about what is good for spiritual health unrelated to somebody's desire for personal gain. Anytime you are learning a spiritual teaching, it is helpful to continue to study other materials so that you can be sure not to become biased or distorted, and so that you can keep your mind open to what is beneficial to you. Do this whenever you cannot decide whether a teaching is virtuous and upright or not.

Let us talk about some basic points of religious teaching. Confucius promoted the Tao of five relationships. The first relationship is filial piety. Filial piety means being a faithful son or daughter. Being a faithful or obedient son or daughter is a basic practice. It is a way to cultivate Tao. But Tien Tao always quotes the high profound philosophy instead. Confucius also talked about the four virtues and the three obediences of a woman. Confucius said that before marriage, a woman must obey her parents; after she marries, her husband, and if her husband dies, she must obey her son. This is only the surface. They do not look into the deep reality. Any satisfying relationship is a mutual offering of sweetness and kindness. It is not a social obligation. It is personal improvement rather than the demand of one strong or weak side.

Previously, they said a person needed to have three thousand good deeds and eight hundred merits to learn Tao. Now, they say that their followers can learn Tao by paying ten dollars. One follower of this group said," By paying that small amount of money, the heavenly sages and the Buddhas will think you are sincere and come to teach you. Or heaven will change its mind; heaven thinks Tao should be universal, so it teaches everybody. Everybody pays a little money and heaven is going to teach them. The people pay ten dollars to start, that is not too much. Heaven decided that, not us. It is true, heaven decided it. Some would like to pay $10,000. Surely, more is welcome. People think it is cheap, so they would like to learn. After they learn, they would like to pay more. After class, sometimes we give a meal, and also in the altar we need to buy flowers and so forth. It is all decided by Heaven, so you have to follow it."

The leaders of this society have told people that a person who has sexual relationships cannot ascend to heaven. They say that according to the five disciplines of Buddha's dharma, a person cannot have sex. If once they have sex, they cannot ascend, so they become monks or nuns. They say that a person can have sex only if formally married; marriage does not include that discipline. If a person is not formally married, then he or she is sexually guilty. They do not see that marriage is a social formality. The truth of sexual relations is mutual benefit. The undisturbed harmony between the partners in a relationship is heaven. To emphasize sexual self-sacrifice in marriage is unnatural. Thus, it would become a punishment. What Heavenly reward can be received other than the healthy growth of one's children?

Q: The issue of sex and marriage are all tied up together.

Master Ni: Recently there was an Iranian writer who wrote a book. In one part of it, he described Mohammed, the spiritual leader of Islam, whose tenth wife was a prostitute. This description angered the Islamic nation, so the leaders decided to put a death sentence on him as punishment. However, this person did not live in Iran but lived in England and had been naturalized as a British citizen. In truth, Mohammed actually married a much older wealthy widow. According to his own spiritual nature or perhaps because of dissatisfaction in that particular marriage, he devoted himself to staying in caves and rural places to ponder the religious elements of his society. From that, he produced a new book, the Koran, which was a new conception of a unified, strong religion. After he succeeded in making his conception popular, he married several women. I believe he truly knew the need, desire and ambition of the physical body of a man. He also understood that the physical and spiritual are two different things on a worldly level. The harmonious way of marriage should, if possible, be decently, naturally fulfilled on both sides, spiritually and physically.

Do you know how long ago the system of marriage was established? The custom of marriage began on earth around 1122 B.C., when the Chou Dynasty started. Before the marriage system was established, people still had sex, so it could not be that only the people who lived after that and who were married could rise to heaven.

Q: It seems that so many religions, including "Tien Tao", talk about saving the soul. The level at which some people discuss it seems somehow not right.

Master Ni: Some teachings establish a slogan of saving souls. It is important to know if it is just meaningless religious practice or if there is a true reason that souls must be saved. Some groups say that their teaching can save souls. Always ask, how do you save the soul? Is there any true evidence that a soul can be saved? After a person's soul is saved, what does he do? Do people merely become followers and adopt the doctrine that is promoted? Do those doctrines promise that souls can be saved?

If the person has not attained any real understanding or growth and instead just parrots the intellectual material or the dogma he has been shown, then that is not saving a soul. That is merely adopting the externals of a religion.

Pure psychology changes attitudes.   Psychology is different from spiritual growth; it cannot be called saving the soul.   It is true that a positive psychological effect can improve and help people's lives, but that is not spiritual growth.

I have written extensively on the topic of the soul and "saving the soul" in my other books, so rather than repeat information that has already been given, I will refer you to my book *Quest of Soul*, for an in-depth study of this matter so that you can find your own truth.

Q: I have also been to Buddhist groups.   Just as the different groups of Taoism are confusing, the many kinds of Buddhist teachings are confusing to me also.

Master Ni: It is true, there are also many kinds of Buddhism and they can be confusing.   Let us briefly discuss this topic to see if we can understand some of the differences.

I have extensively studied the time in which Buddha lived. The history books say that the Hindu classics built the society that Buddha was born into. This society had developed four strong and different classes. The four classes are as follows: 1) farmers and slaves, 2) business people, 3) soldiers and governmental people and 4) the priests or Brahmin. This is in ascending order with the priests on the top. The four classes could not intermarry. The Hindus built the theory of karma to support their four classes of society. Because the suffering and the enjoyment of each of the four classes is totally different, karma expresses the blessing and reward or misfortune and punishment from one's past life which manifests in this life.

Hinduism started earlier than Buddhism. Hinduism was developed out of people's doubt about their society's spiritual conventions.   One of the conventions in question was the notion that offerings to the spiritual world were powerful and effective in solving human problems. Buddha, who was also known as Sakyamuni, withdrew from general religious teaching. He was looking for the truth of life. Sakyamuni Buddha was a person, but the name "Buddha" means a person of awakening. Sakyamuni took a long time, at least seven years of staying in the forest, to experience what is the mind, what is hunger and what is the desire of life. He knew at least about the basic survival of life. He said the classification of society is an untruthful establishment. He said that all people have a spiritual nature; all people are born equal. This was a great discovery at that time, over 2,500 years ago. Only a great heart and mind can have such a strong vision that sees this truth and make such a discovery. His teaching does not tell about the soul; surely it connects with the soul, but Buddha's new theory that everybody's spiritual nature is equal discredits the standard that society has four classes. His dharma or teaching has three things to worship and five disciplines. The basic elements of Buddhism are: Do not kill life, Do not have sex, Do not drink wine, Do not steal and Do not lie.

Buddha himself did not have such a teaching as saving the soul. His teaching says that people need help from feeling the bitterness of life, being old, sick and dying. It is mostly psychological.

The big vehicle of Buddhism is the later mixture brought about by the integration of the general Indian faith in Hinduism and Buddhism. They were put together as a new Buddhism which became popular in northern Asia. The karma theory was readopted by the teaching of the big vehicle. This occurred after the southern teaching received the influence of the northern teaching. Those scripts were presented much later than Buddha's lifetime, so they cannot be thought to be the genuine teaching of the original.

Tibetan Buddhism taught about the jong ying sin, the life of the middle stage after death and before rebirth, which you call the soul. This means when the bodily life ceases, there is an in-between stage before the life is totally scattered, but there is no permanent existence. That is part of new Buddhist teachings which are against original Buddhism. The followers of Tibetan Buddhism believe when their spiritual leader dies, he will immediately be reborn and again become the political and religious leader of Tibet. So after his death, the followers immediately begin to look for the newborn baby who came to continue the position. This baby is believed to be the reincarnation of the last soul. Tibetan Buddhism says that in this life each follower is going to be Buddha. It is totally a personal achievement.

General local Buddhism teaches the level of karma. For example, it says that a woman needs three lifetimes of being a good person, then she can change to the male opportunity. So that must mean a woman needs another two lifetimes to do it, assuming that this is the first of the three.

In general, Buddhist teaching thrived by teaching the theory of karma. But the deep sense of the theory of karma is not to teach karma. It would rather talk about the liberation from karma. That is the only true value of teaching karma. My impression is that what they talk about only picks up the frame of Buddhism in talking about three lives: past lives, the present life and future lives. The same is true of karma and the law of cause and effect. Also, if karma is all the truth, people do not have any responsibility for their bad fortune or bad behavior because it is their past life karma. This is a total misrepresentation of Buddhism.

Hindu popular beliefs say if a person was born a slave or farmer, or has hard labor and a bitter life, it is all his karma, so he does not need to improve it. In such case, he has not really dissolved his life and death, so he needs to come back again. But they say you need to wait for the reward in the next life. When a person has a next good life, does he eat meat? Does he live in a good house? If he does, then these are all the things Buddhists believe to be immoral.

Buddhism became established in China more than 1,000 years ago. Buddha's teaching was only about general life and how to regulate the mind. Buddha was not one to talk about any problem of the soul, so the teaching of saving the soul is not his creation. Saving the soul is the creation of a new doctrine. Talking about the soul or reincarnation comes from general Hinduism. It is different from Buddhism.

The society of "I Guan Tao," or "Tien Tao" as it is called now, uses magic writing and says that all sages, including Buddha, Jesus or Mohammed, come to talk and to support what their group is doing. Objective-minded people know that magic writing is a kind of skill or trick that this group plays with. Thus, "Tien Tao" also teaches Buddhism through magic writing. The magic writing claims that this Buddha comes, that Buddha comes, this sage comes and that sage comes. It is clear that this is a total lie. It is all human fabrication. Maybe the group leader received some inspiration or admires the sages, but all in all, he needs to take responsibility for what he does. Nothing Buddha discussed connects with what the general teachers of "Tien Tao" or any similar level of religion say.

Buddha himself did not use a so-called karma theory to support his teaching, but his name and teaching is sometimes twisted by monks and nuns who make their religious life into a profession so they can ask for donations and alms from other people.

Q: This group uses magic writing and the person says that the messages from the magic writing change people's lives. Master Ni, is magic writing truthful?

Master Ni: Magic writing is a tool used by "Tien Tao" and other religious groups. They say the magic writing gives a message from the departed souls who were believers in their group and who are happy on the other side. Let me ask you: Do those souls still feel the threat of Communism? Do the souls still need to worry about taxes? Do the souls still need to be afraid of the social customs of marriage and divorce and so forth? Do the souls still need to be anxious about promotions, raises, not enough income and so forth? What trouble do they have?

The small island of Taiwan has a thousand big and small temples. Each temple has a channel or magic writer. All of them have spirits in different temples who give different messages. If it is the exclusive privilege of the departed souls of their group to have more enjoyment, can those souls freely enter the other magic writers to give messages? Why is it that only the ones who are trained in their group do their magic writing and give their messages?

I cannot say whether magic writing is truthful or not, but I do not think it is reliable. I would like to give you an example, from a group in Kao Hsiung, a city in south Taiwan.

Magic writers are usually young people. Once, a magic writer had some conflict with the tien chuan shr, the title of the local main teacher. So this young magic writer used his position and a past master's name, Chahng Tien Ran, to scold the local teacher. Then the local teacher, who was more powerful because of his position, kicked the young man out. However, the young man later received some money from the teacher, because the teacher was afraid of damage to his spiritual group's reputation if the secret of the false magic writing became known. To keep the young man from revealing the secret, the local teacher gave him money. That young man, with the help of that money, ran a bookstand on the streets of Kao Hsiung city. I knew about those events because my uncle was a customer at the bookstand at that time.

The magic writing is usually done by young children. The children have a much looser mind, so its cyclic capability is easily conducted and released. When they do magic writing, they can know what comes as a subtle impression or what you think about in that moment.

Q: Master Ni, the thing that troubled me about the "Tien Tao" was their claim that the world will come to an end. They say that the world is about to go into the third stage, which is total destruction. Is this true?

Master Ni: They declare that, "Now we have come to the third stage of destruction. The entire world will be destroyed. At this time it is important to save your soul through us." So now it is the third stage of total destruction and the only possible hope is through their salvation. We never heard Confucius say that, nor Lao Tzu or any other teacher. Maybe we have a different perception but no one of the great originators of religious paths say that. Who started saying it?

In my understanding, it was written on a piece of carved stone found on the shore of the Yellow River after the establishment of the Republic of China by Dr. Sun Yat Sen's revolution. I have a photograph of that carving. I showed it to a young student, but he did not like to look at it. He said he could write ten thousand pieces like that; it is human writing.

There is a story written about a group of bandits. The bandit was the type of person who would not obey anyone else. One day, some people saw firelight on the land. When they went over there and dug a hole, they found a carved stone. The stone had the names on it of all the people in the community. On it was a written order stating who were supposed to be the leaders and who were to be the followers. It demanded that all the people obey this order.

I do not think that anyone should use something like this as "proof" to make other people follow. They assert that no human wrote it and that it was a heavenly gift to the world. All of their people insist that it is heavenly work. How can anyone know whether it was heavenly writing? Why did heaven use human language, especially the Chinese language? It sounds like another version of the ten commandments, but in Chinese. So that is where this writing about the destruction and the salvation originated.

The leaders of "I Guan Tao" explained that the first period is called Ching yang, the green sun period. The second period is the stage of red sun. Now it is the time of the white sun, the third stage.

They claim that a period about 5,000 years ago was the stage of green sun. The worship for that time was to stand with one palm in the center of your body as a salutation or greeting. Then came the hong yong chi, the stage of sunshine, when both palms were held together in the center. Now it is the time of the white sun. The white sun worship is this way, holding your fist.

At the ching yung, or green sun time, it was Sakyamuni Buddha's legendary teacher who first lit the lamp. This teacher was known as the Buddha of lighting the lamp. When the time of the red sun came, Sakyamuni was the Buddha. Now this supposed third stage is the white sun, when Maitreya becomes the authority.

It is supposed to mean that the Buddha of Lighting the Lamp was the authority over earth in the first stage, Sakyamuni Buddha was the authority of earth in the second stage, and the Maitreya will be the authority in the third stage.

The teachers of the group declare that the origin of their teaching is Fu Shi, Lao Tzu, Confucius, Buddha and Hui Neng. In fact, this theory of the three stages of destruction is not found in any of their teachings.

The Tien Tao people also like to quote a scripture which says that nothing lasts forever. Do they truly understand this? If they really understand this, then why do they need to establish their teaching of the so-called third stage of total destruction? Any moment, any time or sense, is already in the stage of constant change. They do not need to invent a first stage, second stage or third stage. Neither is there is any way to establish what is saved, who is the savior or what has been saved. This is not the truth nor is it a foundation or motivation for spiritual realization or for giving spiritual help.

So, each moment everything is constantly in change. This is already described in the *Book of Changes*. That group utilizes the psychological effect of this to preach doomsday. It is clear that the group takes advantage of people who feel they have lost their way in life by threatening their minds and causing them to depend on a more powerful message to "help" themselves.

They do not say that the lost soul will be gained and what is saved will be lost, because everything is changeable.

Q: Could you explain what was referred to by green sun, red sun and white sun?

Master Ni: About the theory of the sun, the stages of green, red and white sun were the discovery of the ancient developed people. They knew that the life of the sun has stages just as the life of a human occurs in three periods, youth, middle age and old age. The sun is now still in the middle stage of its life. Its old age, and its exhaustion, will come in around 100 million years. This is no threat for humans because they can prepare themselves spiritually by transforming from the formable level to the formless.

The ancients taught about these stages, but the teaching has been twisted and misapplied by the leaders of this group. The ancients made such an interesting understanding of nature, but I Guan Tao twisted it into a bizarre understanding of nature. They interpreted this great knowledge into the meaningless ritual changings in the smallness of social folk religion establishment. This group of people believe that in the third stage, a big catastrophe will come to the world and end the life of humans. The actual meaning behind this concept of the three stages of the sun is much more useful than predicting a catastrophe. It is illustrated by the system of the *I Ching*, which develops the theory of three stages. The ancient wise ones observed that anything in its first stage of growth is just starting as the beginning. When the long preparation of the first stage is done, the second stage or good time is coming. It is a time when great fruition is seen and reached. The third stage is the time of excessive expression, like the downfall at the end of an arrow's flight.

This is illustrated by the bottom trigram in each hexagram of the *I Ching*. In the 64 hexagrams, the third line mostly expresses excessiveness, being worn out, insufficiency of effort, unachievement, disappointment, being too late to achieve and so forth. Two most valuable books in Chinese culture, the *Tao Teh Ching* and *The Golden Means*, both were derived from the *I Ching*. Both books teach balance and undisturbed natural growth of the individual and avoidance of extravagance and violence. This is because in this second stage, one needs special control to lengthen one's prosperity and make a gentle shift to the fourth line which is the beginning line of the second trigram or big stage.

Q: Master Ni, would you explain more about the theory of development of the human world from your view?

Master Ni: There is unlimited potential for development which can be divided into many big stages, but each stage forms a complete wave with low, high and falling curves. If the rising slope is too steep and too high, a possibility that the third stage will sharply plummet is created.

The wise one learns from the great illustration of the *I Ching*, which explains almost everything in the world in an abstract way. So, the wise ones manage their lives to maintain gentle progress, and avoid experiencing peaks, deep ravines and sharp changes. Those types of extremes are not the best for most people's nervous, mental and spiritual systems.

The leader of that Tien Tao group promotes that there will be a worldly catastrophe. Because world trends are in different stages, there is always some potential crisis of human society on the downslope ready to happen. The pivotal point that changes this so that disaster does not happen is the mind. When people turn to the right path of life, correct their mistakes, moderate their emotions and behavior and improve their attitudes towards the external and internal worlds, they find their own salvation.

But this group is not able to do that. They merely make people avoid all kinds of responsibility, and change into religious followers. This is not correct spiritual education for society or for any individual. The authority for saving one's self or saving the entirety of human society is the normalcy of the individual and the general good condition of human society. Is not health and the way of balance the solution? In this group, no correct, meaningful education is given to individuals and society. The teaching of inward withdrawal is not helpful. The only helpful spiritual work is to guide the individual and the human society to grow enough and be able to manage all kinds of crises in their lives.

Q: One person who follows religious teachings told me, "Many people who drink or have smoked a long time join our group and they quit their bad habits. Those people are true followers, they cry in Buddha's Hall. The new believers mention that in their whole life they never heard such a wonderful teaching, so good, so nice. They think it is a proof of how good and how strong their Tao is."

Master Ni: Many religions "help" people by using the sense of guilt; their followers use the sense of immorality and the sense of sin to affect themselves. Many other religions have changed people who adopt their discipline. You cannot say that other religions cannot produce such effects. Practically, it is clear that there is nothing to be proud about. It is not Tao or nature; it is relative human experience of life.

You must understand that religious experience, religious emotions and religious motivations are universal. It is not that any religion is better than others. What one religion talks about should not reject the others. But each religion always uses other religions to support itself at the same time it expresses its main promotion which is not practically relevant with other religions. Then, what is called the United Religions?

Q: That group says that they make people understand to love and take care of themselves. Then why do they charge each person to join the group? Each person that joins must pay a certain fee called a fee of merit to support their group. Why do they demand that people vow? As "If I am disobedient to the teachers, I will die bitterly. Then our heaven will kill me, earth will kill me, people will hate me." Why do they need that vow? Is this a gang or a religious path? This is what I am asking.

Master Ni: Some religions require that a person cast a strong binding vow. Quite often, the people who follow any religion are illiterate or uneducated and do not understand the words, much less the spiritual reality behind them. The teachers lead the followers to believe that if anybody rebels, heaven will kill them and earth will destroy them. People respect heaven and earth, so they are afraid to doubt that. Once they join, by the binding vow, they dare not say anything. Not only that, but the group finds other ways to make people pay for things, so they can get lots of money.

Doesn't the Bible say that each person needs to pay 1/10 of his income to the church? I think now you understand; they are not only Buddhist, they are Christian too. The teaching of their society, like some other religions in the world, is a mixture of the practices and understandings of different religious traditions. In China, there were many folk religions and rebellious activities throughout many generations. The first teacher of I Guan Tao took all the attractive things that had been used before. Now they have become the burden of the new teachers because all these earlier teachings were undeveloped.

However, each type of religious teaching serves a different category of human need. Different teachings should not be confused. It wasn't that at the beginning of this society there was a meeting of the leaders of each tradition and they decided to combine them. New organizers certainly have the right to combine something if the elements are correctly understood. Especially, a teacher who is an initiator of new teachers must have a special achievement. A responsible teacher needs to make it clear that, "I have organized those teachings; I adopted this from here and this from there for my own learning, and I have achieved this combination, etc.

Q: Master Ni, there is a lot of talk about different heavens. Could you please clarify this point that is so confusing.

Master Ni: One must attain Tao; then anywhere can be heaven. Heaven is not an after-death place of imaginary glory.

The initiators of the group talk about the heaven of ultimate truth and the heaven of law. It is clear that they do not know, practically, what that means. Truthfully, each individual is one possible heaven. As the proverb says, above each individual's head there is a heaven. This proverb promises individual spiritual future. This proverb also indicates that the development of each individual can be different. If a person successfully cultivates Tao, he does not wait until a next life to do better.

To me, the next moment or next day also can be recognized as the next life, because life is renewing itself as a nonstop, ongoing process. In the ultimate heaven, I do not believe that there is a life or a death to be dissolved. But they talk about life and death as two separate things. To me, there is no extant separation.

Where is ultimate heaven? The leaders of this group say the person who has become achieved from his worship is going to ultimate heaven. Why, then, can the achieved ones who are in the ultimate Heaven be manipulated by the magic writers?

This society talks about the heaven of law, the heaven of form and the heaven of energy. It is chi. It is a metaphor to describe the human body.

Q: What is the Maitreya? Is it someone who has already come or someone who is supposed to come in the future?

Master Ni: The true Maitreya was the Hindu sage of later generations. Maitreya was a person like us, you and me. He was an author. He spoke about how the human senses and mind relate to the content of personal knowledge. That was his fundamental theory. Not he himself, nor anybody later, thought he would wish to have authority over the human realm, or to become the human realm at all. Maitreya may be considered as the first person to establish the shape of science as psychology.

He identified eight senses. The first five senses are seeing, hearing, smelling, tasting and touching. He added a sixth sense, which is the combination of the five, the seventh sense, which is the self or ego, and the eighth sense, the essence. The eighth is the most subtle, it is the seed of the mind that carries all the memories of the past lives. He never said anything about Heaven in his teaching.

Nobody has seen his image, and in ancient time no picture was shown of Maitreya. But in China, the promoters of Zen Buddhism speak of a spiritual person called the monk of Big Bag who appeared on a bridge of Ning Puo in Chechiang province and played with the children. They created an interesting image. This image does not connect with the real author, the Indian philosopher, his teaching or anything else. There is no real connection.

Q: Master Ni, the other thing I found confusing was talk about heavenly law. This is what they told me: "Tao is magic. Tao is magic writing. A person has to fulfill the way of heaven, the Tao of man. You must follow the regulation and the social code of society. Also we need to fulfill the heavenly way. Once you fulfill the heavenly way, you will see the heavenly law."

Master Ni: Different persons with different educations and different minds view heavenly law differently. The human mind is not the heavenly law.

The leaders of this group say that because we have reincarnated so many times, we do not know heavenly law or god any more. They say that before we were one way, and now we are another way. Thus they say that the soul, the spirit or god is changeable. Or that so many years ago God was that way, many years later God is this way. This is what they said. Then what is saving the soul? Are they saying that many years ago people were part of God and now they are not?

Q: Master Ni, would you talk more about the stone carving of the teaching of I Guan Tao. It was said to be discovered many years ago during a time when the bank of the Yellow River collapsed.

Master Ni: I myself read that piece of writing. The style of writing which was carved on the stone is not the work of a highly educated person. The level of this piece mostly pretends to confirm that the leader of this quasi-religious society has authority from Heaven. The style of writing is similar to the magic writing of the Chinese who did not receive a good education. In Chinese standards, this piece of writing is not of high quality.

However, because the younger generation lacks education in traditional Chinese literature, they are too ready to accept it. They lack the education to understand the level of this irresponsible game that has been played on the general public so many times throughout history.

Advice from Master Ni:

There is danger in this kind of grouping. Historically, they have used the names of the already accepted sages to make their own teachings acceptable and agreeable. Then, in their own teachings and talking, if they are 95% right, a follower's rational scrutiny will not notice that 5% is wrong.

The minds of most people cannot discern it. Taking the example of Jim Jones, I do not think he could put seven hundred people to death in New Guinea by poison without their willingness. It was the trust he built up day by day; a high percentage of his talk was agreeable and reasonable to the general mind and made people trust him. Trust is the faith you have built in a person. In his case, he suddenly changed and people did not notice because of the trust or faith built over a long time. A quasi-religious society can utilize 95% of what the sages say and mix 5% into it which is not true, and people never notice it. This causes trouble.

They have strong faith in what they believe, although it is untruthful. We also see that the extremists will give up their friends who have different beliefs. If these extremists feel that they find sweetness there in their particular group, they often will not find anything interesting in their own family, or among friends, because their levels are so different. However, they claim that they are happy as a result of joining the group.

Happy or unhappy, saved or unsaved, there is still only one true way. The true way is self cultivation. Surely, anybody who superficially talks about cultivating Tao but in reality continues to brew poisons such as aggressiveness, greed, hatred, prejudice, attachment and insistence, finds that those things become the trap of his or her own soul.

Sometimes a group successfully builds an emotional connection with those who feel rejected by general society, or are not 100% satisfied with their connections in the world. A feeling like that creates a vulnerability to religious schemes. It shows the undevelopment of the human mind.

Now there is this problem: the teachers who are active in the western community especially welcome the overseas Chinese who do not have a deep understanding of Chinese culture. Then through them, they influence their western friends. That is a bad beginning, although it is a powerful, influential approach.

From my viewpoint, I believe one's own personal achievement is the real achievement. Anything that causes you to depend or rely on something else is not a truthful teaching. Other religions say, join us and learn from us to attain Tao.

No, to attain Tao is to be spiritually independent, not dependent on salvation or anything else. Tao is the one road. It is a road from which you can be a sage. It is a road paved by your own spiritual nature.

History does not determine the future. As the Chinese proverb says, a noble person can be born in a humble hut. A butcher who stops killing can bear spiritual fruit as good as Buddha's. A prostitute, once she stops her habit, can achieve as highly as a saint.

Looking at society, we can see that all matters follow the principle of economics: where there is a need, someone will supply what is needed. If something is not needed, it will not prosper. Thus, we see that all religions and all teachings have a good reason for their existence. They can be helpful tools for people. It seems that the masses of humans still have need of policemen, criminal courts, judges, lawyers and the religious stories of heaven and hell. Although the entire human society is making progress, it is not as fast or immediate as developed people could wish.

All different folk religions, including this one which you are interested in, begin with a mixed purpose. Right or wrong, each teacher gives a presentation according to his or her understanding and according to what fits with the needs of society. In the past, people's emotional life was suppressed by the dictatorship of the government. Now, politics have changed, but life pressures still exist. There is one fact that needs to be recognized in spiritual teachings: as the world situation changes, teachings also change to adapt to that new situation. All teaching is subject to such a principle. If 5,000 years ago I came along to teach Taoism, I do not know if anyone would feel interested in the subject of being natural and original as useful guidance. All of our ancestors were more original and natural than any later teacher. I still have my hopes that everything will change positively, including even evil things in the world. Surely this includes the positive change of this society.

Q: This was an interesting discussion, but mostly you are talking about the past. How does this relate to a modern person's life?

Master Ni: I have a number of things to say in response to this question. First of all, from looking at all of this, we see that human spiritual life is necessary, but religions can be a false lure. Although religions offer a certain fashion about spiritual life, they cannot assist the real spiritual growth of people. We can, however, take lessons and learn from all religions to find a better way for our own spiritual cultivation. We are at a vantage point of being able to examine all of the religions.

Let us look at the teaching elements that the leader of I Guan Tao has taken in. Confucius' teaching, which is the foundation of the Chinese social system, should be basically discarded, because monarchy and the big family system no longer exist. Nobody will go back to enjoy living in a big agricultural community where their own labor produced the means of survival for the folks in one family. Confucius' teaching supported the family system. Families are of course still relevant to modern life, but not as he taught. I do not think those particular customs are truly healthy to modern life.

Confucius' teaching especially supported loyalty to the monarch. It taught that one must sacrifice oneself and even die in offering one's loyalty to the monarch. I do not promote that type of thing. The reason that the originators of this religion picked up Confucianism was because they wished to establish a monarchy, that is, a dynasty. That is not spiritual progress. Truthfully, that is not even spiritual teaching at all.

The leaders of I Guan Tao also chose the big vehicle of Buddhism rather than the small vehicle to suit their political purpose in order to reach the vast public. The so-called small vehicle is like a car that can only take a few people. It is strict, not many people are involved with it. The big vehicle can take many people; they go to work on the masses, and some depth is lost. The big vehicle changes the original philosophical type of teaching to more religious teaching. It gives the general public an emotional lure.

The true Chinese Buddhist is a student of Chuang Tzu, looking for the transcendental truth which is unspeakable. Anything that can be spoken of or on a narrative level, is not the way to touch the highest, transcendental truth. However,

I Guan Tao combine their teaching process with the big vehicle teaching. So first they spread the sickness, then they give people the medicine. I mean, they first teach you the shallow religion, then they are going to enlighten you. This process is not what I adopt.

They also take in what was originally from the teaching of Manichaeism, the teaching of becoming vegetarian. In Manichaeism, the main slogan is to conquer satan by eating vegetables. This means that people who eat vegetables will decrease their sexual desire and easily handle themselves. But, let me ask you, who is satan? It is clear that satan is a part of oneself. Mani established a high moral standard; I have personal respect for him. He also emphasized the four virtues of purity, lightness, wisdom and power. I would like to have those things too. Though they are secondary merchandise, and are still not the depth of spiritual teaching, they are still a good thing. Why do I say that it is a secondary teaching? Because it is still relative. Purity is associated with impurity, light with darkness, wisdom with stupidity and power with weakness. It is all relative, however, he liked to relate to the light side of the world, of human nature. I welcome it, though it is a secondary teaching. It is not thorough. But, Mani's life or teaching had a high moral standard compared to many religions. It shows no less value than any religion. This group still worships the God of Light, the Illumined One, in Chinese as "Ming Ming San Ti."

So this is the main teaching of this group, Tien Tao. But one other thing they particularly mention is the theory of the messiah. There are two messiah theories that we know about, although perhaps there were many that no longer exist. Jesus was popularly considered as a messiah, or at least the Church preached that he is. Buddhism preaches that the Maitreya is a messiah. So let us discuss this topic. These thoughts of having a messiah come from the desperate emotions of people who are looking for a replacement, a change, or external strength to come to save them. It was cleverness on the part of the ancient spiritual leaders to project such thoughts. Practically, a change can happen; a better replacement can be made, but it happens spiritually. It can only be done individually. If you keep expecting Jesus or Maitreya to come to help you, you are following somebody else's ideas. Even if a strong leader type were to come and succeed in changing the world, he could still not change the reality of you. A person does not change unless that individual becomes his own messiah. I am talking differently from the way Mani taught. Mani said we need to conquer satan and conquer the darkness. But as I have pointed out, satan is your own improper desire; the messiah is also your own hope. Nothing can help the reality of an individual or the world unless each individual improves his own spiritual quality to make a world composed of refined, achieved individuals. Then the heavenly paradise or the heavenly kingdom can be realized in the world.

Now I would like to give you the lesson we can learn from spiritual groups. The first thing is that a spiritual group or teaching has got to have a pure motivation, and not get involved with the mundane issues or conflicts of the times. The mundane life of politics is not a thorough solution. Secondly, a spiritual group should not be mixed up with political ambition. Spiritual achievement and political achievement are different. Political achievement offers a good administration when there is a specific problem. Some hero type of leader or some hero type of group comes to help. However, as history has shown, that group or leader also creates a side effect problem for other people to fix up. So as I view it, political solutions are never the fundamental way of spiritual improvement. The fundamental improvement, as a spiritual person, is to work in the long purposed goal. Start from oneself and reach out to do whatever one can do in the world.

Worldly life and society are like an ocean. Before, people used small, individual canoes in the water, which was dangerous. Later, they began to use a boat, then a ship, and now today's luxury liners are much improved. But the ocean is always the ocean; it has its own, same nature. It is the humans who have increased their skill and knowledge of water, climate and so forth to make travel safer. That is all there is to it.

So living a good life has got to be concentrated on for the improvement or progress of the individual. We can learn that external effort such as that presented by religions usually creates an emotional support, but in reality, no change occurs in the world.

The minor practices of eating vegetables or having no sex are wise, but they cannot be a standard for looking down at other people as unholy. Some people consider others who eat meat as unspiritual, or that there are certain sexual practices that are unholy. Spiritual pride is not an achievement. I do not reject those practices at all; I still have respect for those who reduce personal enjoyment to be vegetarians or to be celibate, but that is personal choice, not universal truth. That is not a standard that can be established to determine holy or unholy, spiritual or unspiritual. I recommend that all of you, if possible, eat properly and if possible, keep your good energy. That is my main suggestion.

In this long talk we have learned many things. So if we have anything to offer to our friends, if we are going to teach, do it with sincerity, or give advice as a service, we do not use a special skill like magic writing to control people's minds. Genuine magic writing does not establish any well known spiritual personality as the authority or source of its writing, but only gives the service. Knowledge is of two kinds: one kind is mental, we perceive a sense; we know a thing. If we do not perceive it, we do not know about it. Knowledge of spirit is intuitive, it is straight; it is just known. Spirits do not know why they know. They do not need to use a chart, read a book, sort through information, obtain data or start a computer. They just know in that second, that we need that kind of service. That is helpful, that is respectful. Unfortunately, magic writing has become a trained skill with the purpose of teaching and controlling the believers. When I was young, I saw many people doing magic writing in a sandbox; this means, people were doing magic writing just for fun or to answer a question. Sometimes it was very inspired and a beautiful poem came through. It is all natural communication; unfortunately, it becomes organized and therefore spoiled by religious purpose, whether it is a good purpose or bad purpose.

Opening the mystical pass is a ancient, valuable spiritual discovery which can help a spiritual person, in his due time, to exuviate from the body. This service, taken from the tradition of Tao, was a secret in ancient times. By this service, those original souls recognized their own path back to the spiritual origin. The seeds of eternal life just means the yang energy of nature. I believe that to the one who is searching spiritually, spiritual support is more than just emotional support. The way of organizing or grouping people may offer some emotional help and also an opportunity to learn from each other. That is something that can be done naturally, however, and not necessarily by participating in a particular group.

An achieved teacher can do this service of touching the mystical pass in any occasion, any time the people request it, without charge. The receiver of this service does not need to be a member of the group or a student of the teacher. This selfless spiritual service can be given to anyone who is looking for it, without establishing any personal extension of power over any person. I do it myself and I have also authorized you to do it for free. I also recommend that any of you can help each other and help yourselves to receive the benefit of this practice. It is outlined in the books, *Quest of Soul, Nurture Your Spirit* and the *Workbook for Spiritual Development of All People.* But do not forget that one's general spiritual preparation is more important than just having an unchanged color and soft corpse during your exuviation. Virtuous fulfillment comes from an upright personality and life; that is the ladder going upward. Ascension is not accomplished by doing any external ritual, or being controlled by a particular group.

So this is my personal response to the question you have asked. Personally, although I enjoy doing the service, my own enjoyment is in the following type of message which is called "No hour and no day."

In all circumstances, I respond to your questions and to what you need to know. I still have my own spiritual enjoyment, the heaven of the ultimate truth. I would like to show you, which may tonify your marrow.

1

No hour and no day.
The subtle truth cannot be seen
   by one who is searching for it wildly.
It is truthful as it is at any time.
In his wild search, he does not know
   the treasure is as near as his own palm.
Once he thinks he has caught something
   that is truth,
   he has only run into a puzzle in his mind.
Whatever he values obstructs his vision.
Do not insist on believing that truth has no form;
   it is just unable to be seen
   by undeveloped eyes.
No need to search for knowledge
   that is attained by learning.
It is still far from the subtle truth.

2

No hour and no day.
When the subtle truth is put into use,
   there is no use of special skill.
Let the subtle light
   reach the fact of all things.
Extra use of the mind
   will invite the devil's trial.
If you are going to do something
   to enhance your mind's search,
   you will reach nowhere.
Instead, you only become obstinate and awkward.
Do not apply an analytical approach
   to a life situation,
   but just keep on flowing.
Then, no trouble is created for your mind.

3

No hour and no day.
Darkness is the foundation of becoming wise.
The truth is as straight
   as the simple action of sitting or laying down.

Don't bother with all the trouble of finding it.
Listening to sound and watching color,
and distinguishing the relationships
of who, what, when, where and how
are all still external matters.
That is only brushing on paint to color the mind.
If you use your conceptual beliefs
as truth for uplifting your soul,
you just plant yourself deeply in the fire.

4

No hour and no day.
There is no way to teach people
who have not reached where they could be,
even if they understand
all the important instruction
from truly achieved ones.
It is no good to think
you are the one who understands the truth.
Keep to the subtle truth,
which cannot be carried by words.
To recognize it in one way or another is still not right.
Once you have reached it,
there is no need to search further.
This way, there is no Satan
to trouble you on your way.

5

No hour and no day.
That is the priceless treasure
grown from the body which is composed of
earth, water, wind and fire.

You do not like to give up playing with
fireworks of world glamour.
If you think you can find a way to make it everlasting
by your religious faith,
you have become lost.

You take the paint for enlightenment.
It is the ruin of all good days.
In the formed body,
    exists the natural unformed essence.
In the dark journey,
    exists the essence of needless rebirth.
Why do you allow the cunning minds
    of the leaders of religion
    to play on your psychology?

6

No hour and no day.
There can be no pre-established understanding
    toward the subtle truth.
All good teaching from writing or speeches
    is an interpretation and not directly
    the subtle truth.
No need to work meticulously on the words
    to get the truth's exact description.
Roam where no obstacle arises.
Abolish all superstition as prohibition.
By living this way,
    you always live with natural vitality
    though you may not live in the limited world.
Natural truth cannot be used
    separately from formed life.

7

One who learns Tao is not dissatisfied
    with his situation in life.
All things which are formed are temporarily gathered.
The unformed essence does not need you to look for it.

People spend years struggling between what is spiritual
    and what is secular.
It is all self-trouble.
They are proud of their foolishness.
Fools keep to the frames of teachings.

The teaching of subtle truth cannot be heard
    by formed ears.
You can call it temporarily
    as the transcendental passage.

8

No hour and no day.
Voiced teaching cannot last.
Do not attach to the feast of festivals.
Stop drinking wine offered
    by those religious celebrations.
Spiritual success cannot be given free.
Neither can it be maintained
    among those foolish activities.
The subtle truth reaches everywhere
    with boundless freedom.
You may even be someone
    who is knowledgeable
    among all people who have lived.
However, you may still be the one
    who is wandering crazily outside the walls.

9

No hour and no day.
The wild boy returns to his own dark room.
Though you can reach the truth of no boundary,
    it makes no difference from what you are now.
Once you decide to think over what is truth,
    you are being the opposite.
That makes your mind as dark as black paint.
The subtle light radiates day and night
    to shine upon what is there and what is not.
Yet, fools call it the path of soul delivery.

10

No hour and no day.
The harder you try,
    the farther you travel from truth.
Once the ambition of learning spiritual truth is gone,
You start to enjoy freedom in the light of truth.
You have surpassed the teachers of superficial culture
    who have been before you.
You have achieved yourself,
    more than all sages with great form.
Now even a piece of tiny dust
    can be kept in your eyes.
Unlike the sages
    who made their mental creation as truth.
They did not see the big blockage in front of them.
You may be considered a fool
    with whatever naturalness.
However, you receive respect from
    masters who have achieved truth.

11

No hour and no day.
Looking for peace
    is the experience of life and death.
Life and death do not belong to search.
The subtle law behind them has no writing.
Words of teachers are still external.
To recognize the time before beingness
    is still not the origin.
Truth can be missed
    when a mind is made up for search.
Yet, all trials of life and death will fade away
    for the one who is subtly and gently
    works with natural integration.

12

No hour and no day.
It has been long that
    the far-reaching light is there.
It cannot be found from outside or inside.
In all circumstances, it operates.
No head is seen and no hands are seen.
The earth can be rotten, but it does not rot.
Those who have not reached the Inner Light,
    please harken to me.
See who is the one that keeps the tongue turning
    in revealing such a subtle truth.

13

No hour and no day.
The unformed and the formed are united.
Once the unformed is disassociated
    from the formed,
    the unformed is the same.
The joy of life and sorrow of death is nonsense.
The formed cannot always be formed.
The unformed cannot be forever unformed.
Both are traveling;
    when they meet, there is a marriage.
When they depart from each other,
    there is divorce.
To put the unformed to fight everything
    for the formed is foolish.
To put the formed to worship the unformed
    is separating.
One who reaches the integral truth
    lives a life of natural subtle integration.
This one is balanced by being with the natural truth.
This one subtly guides oneself away
    from all extreme inclinations
    in a life of integral growth.

Chapter 4

Conventional Skills
of Religious Promotion

I

Q: Master Ni, as Chinese, we played magic writing in our village when we were children. How do you think of it as the tool of teaching, now that it is popular among all temples of folk Taoism?

Master Ni: Different religious backgrounds often use special skills or other means to give teachings. For example, Moses used carved tablets to give the ten commandments which formalized a new faith for his people. Magic writing and channeling is one of those skills that Chinese religious leaders often use.

Magic writing and channeling can be a powerful tool although not always a good tool. At the beginning, it was a recreational activity among young scholars or young girls. Later, it opened communication between people and spirits. There is a story that illustrates how even an emperor was influenced by magic writing.

During the Ming dynasty, the emperor supported a prime minister who was cruel. Through forty years the prime minister, Nieng Soun, did many bad things. He made many people suffer, but during the time of his dictatorship, no one could do anything to improve the situation. Fortunately, there was one opportunity.

The emperor asked a magic writer what to do about a certain situation involving the minister. The magic writer said Nieng Soun should be killed. Only through the emperor's trust in magic writing did he do the right thing at the last moment and kill Nieng Soun.

Nobody can say it was a scheme or something similar. People sometimes employ a psychological belief system through an external formality to correct a mistake that one has made oneself.

In a group activity, a less achieved spirit needs the bodily support of the magic writer or channel in order to do the teaching. However, the most active part of the teaching comes from the mind of the magic writer or channel, not from the spirit itself. Thus, I reject this conventional game as a teaching tool.

Magic writing always produces something associated with the activities of the group. They exploit the material of magic writing to brainwash the believers. The believers think the magic writing is the only truth, and that the sages or achieved souls come through the magic writer to give the message. You can give a magic writing to someone of spiritual achievement or someone who has a religious background. They will give you an honest opinion if you wish to hear it. You yourself cannot truly prove if the writings have any connection with the highly achieved past masters. The magic writers who act as teachers use those respected names, but not their teaching. They claim the spirits who cause them to write are acting for your benefit.

Magic writing cannot be trusted. It is a psychic power. It is not popular. It cannot be used as a regular tool for teaching. If it is, it is obviously pre-trained and artificially arranged. Or it is natural psychic energy that can pick up knowledge about somebody. Many children and young adults have it. Psychic energy cannot be called a special gift or power through one's spiritual background. Psychic capability is seen everywhere, even in advertisements for services, whether truthful or not.

In the later time of folk Taoism, some good books were produced by magic writing. This is because the authors had already dissolved their own egos and did not want to give their own names. Also they did not expect or wish to gather favor from anyone. The value of those books can be judged by the usefulness of the works, not by their style or the skill of how they were produced.

However, a true spiritual path is not confused with the mob movement. If it were a responsible path, books could be written by them and they would not need to teach or utilize the big names that are already accepted. People need to take responsibility for the things they do and the words they say.

It is Chinese religious experience that people and some religions use the ancient books as authority. Some folk religions use mediums or channels to establish their spiritual authority. They employ all kinds of story elements to support their teaching. They practice magic writing, whereby certain sages write through the hands of the magic writer. All contradict the original teaching of the sage. Sometimes magic writing is used in public to attack an enemy disliked by the teachers. This tool may involve politics or religious politics. It is not reality.

In Chinese folk religions, magic writing is popularly used as communication between the ascended ones and humans. However, should or can a highly spiritually developed being be manipulated by a magic writer's human mind which has not attained any development? If that is so, what is the value of magic writing in terms of spiritual achievement? Magic writing is totally different from spiritual achievement. Magic writing reflects the movement of spirit through the body of the writer. But it is not a bit of spiritual achievement, even if the words that come through are truthful. People who do or watch magic writing are entranced by the movement of the writing and totally miss the verbal teachings. True spiritual achievement is different from doing or watching a magic writer, because spiritual achievement comes from what a person does and is, not what he is controlled or entranced by.

Magic writing is not deep spirituality. One sage teaches how the human mind develops by one's conscience or consciousness. What a person conceives within the self depends on how the mind develops. A person's life is like a story creation. Judgement, evaluation and the view of the world are all from the formation of the conscious mind.

Many people can do magic writing after training. There is no secret to it. The writing is just a reflection of personal understanding. It is not as most perceive it, unless the writer is preprogrammed. The way to use magic writing is for a person to tell the truth or develop a new idea under his or her own name. People who are too lazy to establish a theory that requires many long discussions take advantage of magic writing. This is the human darkness that plays upon a dogmatic heart and dogmatic establishment.

A normal person who has learned from the truth with his form, this body, also has a spirit. You see only the person's form, you do not see his spirit. But you think that what the person says is ordinary language. How can it be ordinary language? Even ordinary language expresses truth. How can you deny that the ordinary form you have is divine? You may choose to believe only magic writing is divine or holy because it is not written by a pen. The Chinese folks believe that only magic writing is divine or holy. However, an achieved one's written or spoken language that expresses the divine truth needs no particular ceremony. How? In the spiritual realm, divine energy can reach any person at any time; it is not limited to the body of a magic writer or channel. However, most magic writers or channels do not express divine energy, but just the level of discussion of ordinary level spirits, like everyone possesses.

Each person has a body, a form. Each person also has a spirit. Few people can see each other's spirit, and so they cannot see what a person truly is. They only see the form. However, an ordinary form can contain ordinary spirit or divine spirit; you cannot see the difference without spiritual discernment.

Primarily, channeling or magic writing is the work or the reflection of the mind of the channel or magic writer. When a medium or a magic writer is in trance, sometimes a message is truthful, but this does not often happen. When magic writing is used in a religious gathering to stimulate the faith of followers, the messages are prearranged. There is no really new message, but mostly the repeated teaching of the old with new names of deities to refresh people's faith. The so-called new names of deities are names of conventionally accepted authorities such as Buddha, Confucius, Lao Tzu and other heroes of past generations. People think they have become Gods. New names are added such as Mohammed or Jesus and other sages or maybe even a president of the United States such as Roosevelt. The magic writer can use one such name and say this person comes to talk to people through magic writing. Although magic writers or channels say it is Jesus, Mohammed or Roosevelt talking, the Chinese channels or magic writers speak in Chinese, write with Chinese writing and use Chinese concepts. However, most of the channeled material communicates in the manner of the temple or the small sect of the religion of those who do the writing and much of the material channeled promotes the activities of the temple in which the magic writer works.

People who do magic writing cannot distinguish if it is themselves or somebody else who actually does the writing. The material of magic writing is usually associated with the background and education of the magic writer. From the existing material produced by magic writing, an educated person will easily discover that most of the teachings repeat the old books. If any new message is given, it is in an undeveloped style from people without good education. Most people who channel magic writing are not highly educated. However, although contemporary magic writers may have attended good schools, their literary training is much less than the standard of ancient masters now recognized as Gods or Buddhas. And they only take somebody's teaching to be their own. We do not need to judge the motivation behind these religious activities, but such teaching is irresponsible to past master teachers.

The magic writers also act irresponsibly in using their techniques to influence people in important decisions, marriages, businesses and their personal lives. In addition, they utilized magic writing to attack the masters who did not approve of magic writing or the teaching of those groups.

Through my personal research, study, exploration and experimentation, those things cannot be taken too seriously as the reappearance of original souls. It is untruthful to make a really achieved spirit to be channelled as you wish and make the talk and the writing as his result or the fruit achieved by him. The spirit or soul which can be channelled is sometimes depicted as having achieved highly from cultivation, which is usually untrue. Portraying magic writing or channeling as evidence of a person's immortality to encourage followers of a religious group lacks truthfulness. Even if the soul responds, he must fit the mold of the mind belief of the general public because it is the code or means of communication that people have set up. I mean, the soul who appears in magic writing or channeling must teach the followers in a way that fits the religious structure of the channel or magic writer.

The highly achieved ones cannot be commanded or summoned by someone who is spiritually unachieved. If a highly achieved one wishes to communicate with another highly achieved one, communication is direct and done without the formality of a go-between or magic writers. For example, my teachers or advisers can come to me. I can reach them directly if it is a circumstance of perfect natural meeting or union.

My understanding of magic writing is that it only brings about more confusion. I see no real benefit or advantage in it to humanity's spiritual development. This is why I have reservations about magic writing and channeling, although it has been a powerful tool among the Chinese folks.

Q: Master Ni, we are curious about magic writing. Would you explain more about it?

Master Ni: In the United States, channels and magic writers are popular. Guard yourself against being deceived by false channels and false information. Channels misguide people when they say whatever they say is from one spirit. They do not apply established responsibility, they use a spirit to talk about something, and they speak about individual problems or social problems, producing their work but using the channel of a spirit. They are people, just like us; this is no problem for people who have clarity of mind and can examine their work.

Some people cannot accept direct teaching. Channeling or magic writing can be used indirectly to help people accept the teaching at their level. Some channeling or magic writing is poor quality; some is not. It depends on the originating mind. It may have a good purpose, to see the world achieve peace. Truthfully, some human individuals are god; god being a spiritually achieved individual. God is teaching us and someone is teaching God. It is not necessary to channel a ghost or use magic writing to teach you. It is the different form, a different way of presentation that makes people trusting. This kind of technique is used by virtuous ones for a good purpose. It can be misused by unvirtuous ones of bad motivation. Any unvirtuous person can misuse anything.

Even if a person is not ready for the direct path, there are helpful books, virtuous stories and good movies that are inspiring. Healthy energy produces responsible teaching, but not all teaching is healthy.

There are different ways to attain spiritual growth. One way is to do spiritual practice by yourself through your own understanding. At a certain stage in your growth, you realize that you, as a human life, are a composition of different spirits rather than just a single being. Actually, any single being is a unification of different elements.

Another way is to follow the guidance set down by a particular tradition or religion. I, as a boy, came from an old tradition, but I was also curious about other religions. Not only was I curious, I needed to find out in reality. I mean, although I already had a broad spiritual background which allowed me to be curious about other religions. I wanted to discover their reality by personal experience. Through my explorations, I found out that some religions are primarily conceptual force or power which comes from psychology. It is psychological promotion of faith. By using this faith, social force is built. The followers of these religions do not reach deeply into the spiritual level at all.

I looked at other religions too. I discovered that the practices of religion are usually not as earnest, thorough or truthful as traditional Taoist practices. Taoist tradition is matter of fact; you relate with your personal spirits and the spirits in nature. It is not mythological literature. We do have lots of mythology hiding something in the story. Only people who have reached that level of meaning, smile at the stories. It is not the mythology or the story we promote, it is the hidden teaching. The stories we keep are so that future descendants will discover the truth.

Generally speaking, on one level, you make a choice. Your choice depends on your truthful spiritual development, knowing what is the truth of life, nature and the universe. On the other hand, spiritual students need to be open to any practice that can bring them to the highest achievement to reach the truth.

I do not like to be taught second-hand teaching without directly experiencing spiritual truth. This means that if a group of people wish to teach me God, I will ask the teacher, "Do you know God? Have you seen him? Have you reached him? How can I reach him?" Other religions can never satisfy that reality, but from practices passed down by the ancient achieved ones, a person can reach the truth. It is as I have described in my lectures on different occasions and in my different books. Truthfully, God is internal, God is not external. God is a person's own spiritual development. People project their spiritual energy differently. The one who looks for an external god will fail. The one who looks for internal spiritual development will reach the truth and will reach God.

Another way that a person can grow spiritually is in a natural circumstance, where nothing is organized such as social, cultural or religious customs. Then there is nothing to obstruct one's seeing the natural truth which prevails everywhere.

So let us objectively discuss what we observe or gather from the various ways to grow spiritually. We know that each individual has latent spiritual power. Therefore, when you gather the experiencing of natural phenomenon as personal learning, it is important to realize that some of those phenomena might be your latent spiritual powers. In the case of magic writing or channeling, it may not be an external spirit that is being channeled. It could be but it is not always true.

On many different occasions, I have talked to channels. Channeling or magic writing are usually connected with the latent power of a person using it. An observer of the channel or magic writer who is not confused by the speaking or writing can discover that people do have latent spiritual power.

Now let us talk about real spiritual service from a natural spirit. Natural spirits can be human ancestors. It is not harmful for a spiritual student to contact a natural phenomenon, and channel oral conversation, discussion or magic writing. If it is natural and truthful, a person can learn from such a teacher spirit. This kind of spiritual service is common in small farming communities, where people do not have time to learn about high spiritual truth. China, for example, is mostly populated with farmers. Few people have any spiritual experience or development, so each small village usually has a person who has some psychic skills.

Real spiritual channeling can be of good service too. If there are no people available to help a certain situation, channeling or magic writing may be a way to find help.   I would like to give two examples to help you understand.

Around 20 years ago, when I was in Taiwan, I heard about a woman whose husband was a Chinese air force pilot. On a routine flight, his plane disappeared.   There was a possibility that he might have flown to the mainland or to another place, but because no wreckage was found, nothing was certain.   The question of his fate could not be answered by anybody.   In Chinese Taoism, there is a traditional method called "seeing mystical light."   Usually, a bowl of water is placed on a stool, or a white screen is hung on a wall.   The "readers" are a group of children with no sexual experience because they have pure, innocent hearts better concentration and sometimes easily see visions or images.   The woman gathered the neighbor children around a bowl of water and presented her question.   One or two of the children saw an image in the water - a parachute floating over the ocean. Then the women became nervous, and asked what else they saw.   The children did not see anything else.   The answer was sad and complete, and we do not need to dig out the rest. This is one example of a useful spiritual service.

Here is another example.   Once, in Taipei, a man who owned a big business had large amounts of cash and money in other forms, but he did not let any other person know where the money was kept.   He died suddenly from a heart attack, leaving his wife in great financial trouble.   She did not know what needed to be paid or collected or where he kept his money.   He left quite a mess for his widow, which put her under tremendous sorrow and pressure.   Finally, she found somebody who could help her.   This person summoned the soul of the husband and made the soul converse with the wife.   The wife asked the questions and the husband answered, telling her where he kept his cash and important documents, the number to the safe and how to open it, who he owed and how much, who owed him and how much, where the evidence of those transactions could be found and the names of the people who could prove them. Thus, the widow's problem was solved by this service. Can you deny that this was useful? Can you say it was worthless?

Some people do not have a tight spiritual structure, so on some occasions, a spirit will borrow their function of life to communicate with somebody. People pay a little bit and buy the service they need. I do not think there is anything wrong about it, unless an immoral person fakes the situation and tries to cheat people.

Spiritual development is different from needing the services of channeling and magic writing. In an open society, opportunities exist to experience seeing natural spiritual phenomenon. For breadth of understanding it is best if a person contacts a spiritual expression or channelled spirit that comes from a different social or cultural background. For example, a Chinese spirit comes to a Chinese temple, or an Indian spirit descending to a body in an Indian temple will be able to talk only about the same local, national and racial background. Without something different to compare one's past experience, a person will never understand the truth about the spiritual level. It will be confusing. However, to directly reach the truth you need to rely on your own spiritual development. Most people are seduced by the rituals of created religions, or by the colorful culture of a community or society. These religions and cultures are usually confused.

To a spiritual student of objective mind, there are all kinds of opportunities to receive growth from the experience of such things as hypnosis, channeling and psychic reading. I generally have reservations about such things, but if used correctly and positively, they still can be considered as tools to help a person's difficult time. Growth and deep spiritual understanding only comes when you are not caught by those things.

Q: Master Ni, you have published your version of the Book of Changes. I understand that the I Ching originated from Fu Shi. Would you tell us something more about Fu Shi and how the book originated?

Master Ni: The teaching of Fu Shi is concentrated in the *Book of Changes.* Throughout different religions, people have always respected it. It may be possible that some teacher went south to India to teach the general principle of the *I Ching,* but the *I Ching* principle does not stress the sadness of the impermanence of everything. The teachings of the *I Ching* mainly express that nature is a cyclic movement. The religious foundation of the south is the sadness over the impermanence of everything. However, nobody expects troubles, pain or misfortune to be permanent. All things, good or bad, conform to the Law of Changes. As we know from Taoism and the *I Ching,* the world is developing in a rhythmic pattern. Anything with birth must die. Anything that dies must be born again. Even if the world becomes dark, it will become light again. If it is light, it will be dark again. Each person is a part, a branch, of God. Truth is absolute. There is only one truth, and it is always the same. That is why it can be truth.

Some religions insist that Fu Shi's teaching went to India, then from India it went back to China. This is not true, because the *I Ching* has only recently been translated into English and German. There was no translation of the *I Ching* from Chinese until this century. However, this religion as a sect of folk Taoism just used the name; they do not relate at all with the balanced principle of life taught by the *I Ching.* Therefore, it is obvious that what they say about the traditional background is not true. At least the *I Ching* has not been lost in China since the beginning or made a trip; it has always been in China. There is no need for anyone to go to India to learn *I Ching.* The good teaching of Fu Shi and his spiritual descendants can be found in my work, the *Book of Changes and the Unchanging Truth.*

Q: So much of what Fu Shi developed is taught by your tradition.

Master Ni: The Taoist tradition has its roots in the *I Ching* and its originator, Fu Shi.

The Taoist tradition comes through Fu Shi, the Yellow Emperor, Shen Nung and Lao Tzu.

Fu Shi, who is one of the ancient sages, developed herdsmanship. Before him, sometimes people starved, because they could not always catch animals for food when the seasons changed. Fu Shi's very name indicates why he become so respected; it means "to tame the animals" or "tame the herds." At that time, all people relied on meat for their food.

Also, Fu Shi developed the knowledge of good mating by the *I Ching*. It teaches to reach propriety by making proper changes. The *I Ching* does not establish rigid social rules. In a later epoch, Shen Nung developed agriculture. He taught people to use greens and other vegetables to support their lives. This was a main cultural development.

Fu Shi's active time, according to some classics, was 30,000 years ago. Some say it was 10,000 years ago. He was doubtlessly a great leader before the Yellow Emperor and Shen Nung. The Yellow Emperor was about 5,000 years ago, the dawn of human culture. It is hard to believe that at the same time human life was beginning, the idea of doomsday stimulated our initiating spirits. If the doomsday teaching by Fu Shi were truthful, it certainly has not come in the last 10,000 years. Maybe it will never come. Fu Shi's teaching was yin and yang, life and death, that all recycles and no one side alone should be stressed.

Q: Master Ni, what is the difference between Tao and the Heavenly Way?

Master Ni: The Heavenly Way is the teaching of Lao Tzu. There are several simple sentences in the end of his work that suggest how to realize Tao in personal life. I have published a book entitled *The Heavenly Way* which is a collection of Lao Tzu's teachings. Also, a complete version of the Heavenly Way will be available. This teaching is mainly an individual's spiritual self realization; there is nothing about a plan of grouping people as a negative social force. Though this tradition has centers and study groups in different places, its purpose is to help the individual find spiritual friends to help one another attain spiritual development. With mutual help, each individual can become achieved through this way of learning and cultivating. Participation is non-committal; there is no demand or obligation on the part of any individual who is interested in learning this.

Q: Master Ni, how is karma and the teaching of the I Ching related?

Master Ni: Many people do not know why they suffer or why they are so stupid. They do not understand that a self that has performed many bad deeds and mischievous acts in earlier lives comes back to life to pay those debts to society. A person who bears the burden of their debts from other lifetimes, does not achieve as well as other people. This person does not see what was planted in the last life, determines what is received in this life. This person is envious or jealous of other people who do better than he or she does.

For example, some people become rich but a particular man is poor. He does not know why he is poor and he complains. Because he is jealous, he buys a gun and uses it to shoot rich people to get their money. He does it because he does not know the result of his action. If he knew it, he would give up violence and stop robbing other people. He would rather cultivate and improve himself to do what benefits other people.

Because in his last life this man did not learn the spiritual virtue of generosity and did not give help or alms, in this life he is poor. If he had given alms in his last life, he would be rich now. Because wealth or happiness is a spirit, you need to nurture them within. Then, when the right circumstances arise, the seeds will bloom and bear fruit. If this man wishes to get blessings, he must learn giving, then he will have a better life.

Some people think life is so short. They think, "Why should I trouble myself, I should gather myself for enjoyment. Why worry about anything, like tomorrow or next year?"

The *I Ching* does not set up external retribution as do religions promoting the idea of karma. It implies the knowledge of natural rhythms. It does not imply fortune in the sense that astrology does other than internal cause and effect. Each of you is going through life in the way you are drawing it randomly with a pencil. In this sense, you act out your life on your own karmic treadmill, each working it out in your own way. Whatever you believe, which is still external, your true spirit of life is unknown to your mental being. Thus, you need external beliefs. All conceptual beliefs happen within the context of change.

I believe your question is, how can I do well in life? You can do well in life if you study the *I Ching* so that you understand that the nature of life is change. When you really understand that life is change, the changes will not startle you. So when changes happen in your life, you can hold onto your virtue without fail. Your virtue is ultimately more important than the external changes.

It is my understanding that if you wish to improve your life condition and be better, higher, more truthful or more reasonable, you will achieve your goal.

I would like to conclude today's meeting with the following poem:

Tao is unspeakable.
It is the essence before releasing itself.
The one who knows to cultivate Tao does not argue.
He values this transcendental essence
    as the mother of all.
The one who does not know Tao
    keeps searching over the traces.
He does not know that the trace is not Tao.
Tao is traceless
    because it is the simple essence
    before being released.
How can there be any trace?
After it is released, it is the trace.
    Then, it is not Tao any more.
A person who insists on the traces
    which people have left behind them
    is foolish, although he may look wise.
He has missed the simple essence
    that he could just embrace.

Chapter 5

Important Esoteric Points

Q: Master Ni, your kindness is greatly appreciated. We are particularly interested in the esoteric teachings of saving the soul or the self-saving soul, as you might like to call it. Would you tell the secret?

Master Ni: The human body contains three spheres of energy which all evolved from nature. The center line of the forehead is very important; it is similar to a radar station. Each small section of the forehead has a different spiritual significance. The part next to the edge of the hair growth region is called God's hall. The upper tan tien is at the point between God's hall and the Bright Reception Room which is located between the eyebrows. The Bright Reception Room is also called Bright Meeting Room. Some Taoists decided that the mystical point is at the location of the Bright Meeting Room. Some support it to be the middle point between the two eyes. The soul terrace is located three inches in from the Bright Meeting Room.

The forehead needs to be kept clean and not be touched by anybody. Traditionally, the mystical pass is only used as an initiation or an introduction to the student; the so-called opening of the spiritual eye or channel is just the beginning for his future discovery about spiritual reality and communication inside and outside. This mystical function of the forehead is mostly sort of like a spiritual reception station where messages can be received from the spiritual sphere. This area needs to be kept very well; one should not damage or allow it to get dirty.

Opening the spiritual channel or making a connection with a spiritual background, is possible by touching the points of the forehead. However, the benefit or harm depends on who touches you. What is important is a teacher who is going to help you to open these points. If you choose him to help you, you definitely should take a look at his personal moral condition, intelligence, lifestyle, behavior and spiritual achievement. It is true that another human being can help you by touching you at the Bright Reception Room, the point between the two eyebrows and open the spiritual channel. At the same time that the channel is opened, a spiritual connection is made. It will be beneficial if the right person touches and helps you; thus, you have made a good spiritual connection. If the wrong person does it to you, it is a contamination instead of a healthy spiritual connection. I recommend that you do it by yourself as I instructed in the *Workbook for Spiritual Development* and in the introduction of personal practice of soul discovery in the end of the book, *Nurture Your Spirits*.

This touch is meaningful. In China, it is an old spiritual custom; an old, meaningful, useful, effective process. For example, there are three different occasions upon which a person can be touched spiritually. Let us go from a bad example to a good example. In ancient China, criminals could be punished by decapitation if the crime involved murder. In ancient China, the law was usually simple: if someone murdered someone, he had to give his life for the life he had taken. For the bandit who killed people carrying money at the roadside, it was also a matter of capital punishment. Doubtlessly, the law was simple. In ancient times, if it was a good year, such things seldom happened; such an event would be big news to society. In a bad year, such things would happen occasionally.

Each year, autumn was the time to execute the punishment. Punishment was also for educating the public. Not all the criminals were beheaded at once. Those few chosen ones were selected by the mark of a brush: making a dot on the name. That showed who was to be beheaded. Also, the judge who supervised the capital punishment needed to check out if it was the right person or not in each case before making his decision. Maybe it was not always the right person, because they had a different system of deciding guilt. The judge who took the case reported to the emperor, who then decided or agreed with the suggestion of capital punishment by consulting with a different judge. After they decided the criminal was guilty, they took a black ink writing brush to just touch and make a dot on the forehead of the accused to show that he was guilty. This was done with great authority for it was such a serious matter. In bad years with many bad people, this kind of authority of a government official connected with people's life and death. Just one touch decided whether a person was going to be beheaded. It is a bad situation that the forehead was used that way.

The second situation in China relates to a person's death. Usually a memorial or ancestral tablet was made out of wood. When a person passed away, the ceremonial master, who was usually a Confucian scholar, formally wrote the name, position in the family, date of birth and date of death on the tablet in black ink. In that important moment, he used the red cinnabar brush to make just one touch on the wood to make part of the soul attach to the memorial tablet as the new body. The same would happen with a statue of Buddha or any deity. This process of transporting life by the spiritual touch of a human person is effective. The reason is that once a person has died or passed away, there is no longer a living body; that piece of wood is placed to be the new physical being of the one who has passed away. So in the ancestral house or in each family shrine, sometimes part of the soul stays with the memorial tablet. If a person is developed enough spiritually, he can tell if one of the tablets has the soul attached. Whether or not it is attached still depends on whether the timing was right and the right ceremonial master performed with spiritual sincerity.   Surely this type of 'religious' ceremony was symbolic or metaphorical, not literal. So this is the second occasion in which we talk about the power of one small touch.

The third situation is among the Chinese scholars. Their entire life pursuit is the wish to pass the governmental position and share the rulership of the emperor. In order to pass the official examination, they take a long time to prepare and study. The superior official who decides the passing or failing on the general level will use a red cinnabar brush to touch the top of each person's name on the list to indicate the ones who have passed. One touch means the person passed. And for the high examination to determine who goes to assist the emperor, the emperor decided who is first and who is second. Just one touch decided the destiny of the person. Chinese scholars wish the Big Dipper to shine upon them as individuals so they could pass the important examination with high glory. This was not much development of relative religious conception. Because they identify the Big Dipper as the inspiration of literary energy, or they wish their future career shall be bright as the Big Dipper, so they shall have the opportunity of sharing the rulership with the emperor, the one man ruler. It is a great honor for such a young man to be the first or the best.

So therefore, please understand that the authority of touch is meaningful. Depending on who touches another determines the meaning of the touch. Personally I am not against anything. In my personal observation, general religious activities are more or less against people's intellectual development. But as I see it, the development of intelligence and spirituality are very important. The thing I most disapprove of about the activities of that Chinese quasi-religious society are the deceptive means, such as magic writing, and that the material they promote is mixed up.

In another way, I would like to say a perfect teaching might be a system or a school that not only helps the followers to develop spiritually, but also develops their intelligence at the same time, rather than using a false supposition, dogma or bondage. A stiffened doctrine that is untouchable by the believers is harmful to people's growth.

There are two important differences between my tradition and other religions. My tradition started at the babyhood of human life. We cherish and worship the initiative spirit and life spirits rather than the spirit of dying, saving souls and the next life. Other traditions over-emphasize the death side and do not see the birth side. People talk about God, spirits or souls; however, the proper position of all those are what is manifested. What is more important than religious worship is the unity of all individual life with God, spirits and soul within a person's life. To us, an alive human life is with God and spirits. Separation can bring more harm rather than a better situation of life.

There is no value in arguing and dying for religious differences. Because on the spiritual level there is no definite conceptual shape or name, communication can occur directly without any separation between the spirits and the physical sense of people. The fighting that occurs is mostly at the mental level; it is intellectual level fighting. Why do people fight? Because each side holds certain dogmas or religious structures. They consider them as truth. But they are not the absolute truth; each religion is only one of the formalities the ancient leaders used to attract and teach people, positively speaking. The religious teaching is a servant of life. It is a mistake; religious practice has wrongly risen as the master of life. It is unnatural.

As I truly understand, no one thing can be insisted upon as more important than the other. Both the spiritual and intellectual levels are of the same importance to human life, and both can work together practically as one thing. A developing spirit at the same time develops the intellectual strength of a person. They are so closely related. Unfortunately, the old type of religion is against people knowing too much. They do not allow a person to have a second way of seeing things.

Now let me talk about saving souls. Most religion promotes the saving of the soul or the delivery of the soul. Although they term their teaching in that way, perhaps what they really wish is to attract people who lack spiritual awareness. Spiritual awareness is the growth and expression of the health of each individual's spiritual energy. Directly, a person with spiritual awareness means the person has a strong, healthy soul.

Religious teachers say that they can save your soul. Practically, they cannot save your soul; but perhaps they can remind you to keep up your spiritual awareness in your life and activities and to respond to your living environment with spiritual awareness. For many generations, what the sages were really talking about was totally confused. For example, Jesus said that even if can gain the entire world and you lose your soul, what is good about it? That is truthful, but however, what he says does not really mean you lose your soul; it means you lose your spiritual awareness.

All activities in the spiritual, material or physical sphere relate with personal soul energy. The one who has stronger soul energy has stronger spiritual awareness; he knows what he is doing. He will immediately correct any mistake he makes in his behavior, business, personal life, relationships etc. that he has made. He corrects them so that no misfortune could happen to him. He also acts appropriately when a matter affects other people. He can also provide a better, higher vision which is more complete. To have a more complete vision in guiding oneself is dependent on one's personal spiritual growth. This spiritual system and vision is innate but it can be further sharpened. Each individual is born with an innate spiritual system; if and how it is used depends on if an individual learns to sharpen and cultivate it.

The sages say, you shall lose your soul in the pursuit of the comforts of material softness and luxury. With excessive material extension, a person loses the balance of his personality. Because of his lack of spiritual growth, he is not aware of it while being engaged in life. He lacks enough growth of spiritual awareness to be aware of what he is, where he is and what he is doing.

The external teaching of saving the soul may generate attention from people. But mostly the saving of a person's soul is the nurturing of one's individual spiritual awareness. It must be done by each individual; nobody can really help. For example, we know that over-drinking is bad for a person's health, nervous system, heart and so forth, but nobody can force people not to drink. But one can tell them about it. To really stop drinking, the effort must come from the drinker. So once people hear about saving the soul, they trust the teaching. It becomes their misconception that the teaching can save a person's soul. They do not know saving one's soul is an individual matter, an individual's own business. Saving the soul is this: during the process of each moment of your life, you join with your own soul energy. It is letting the spiritual awareness of the individual have a say in each action. This misconception needs to be corrected so that people no longer think that external religion can save their soul. The reality of saving your own soul is the reality of nurturing your own spiritual awareness. It is not external teaching; it is not external measure; it must be done by each individual by himself. This is what I would like to point out for your own examination.

The human body is a trinity: the heaven of law, heaven of chi and heaven of form. When the three energies meet, if they are correctly established, a human being is created. The great Tao does not depart from human life. It is not separate because it is connected deeply with everything. That is why we cultivate Tao; to have the three heavens appear in our body.

Q: Master Ni, how is it that for some people's body after death still remains soft?

Master Ni: When the people who follow Tao exuviate, their body is soft. It is one achievement from spiritual cultivation. It is not that a person can only temporarily maintain the energy center in the head; it still scatters. Once the energy is totally withdrawn, the body will sooner or later harden again. However, the body is finished. The miracle of personal achievement is that he has moved out of the body. You must understand, it is a secret from Taoist teaching. The corpse color does not change and the body is soft. This, at most, proves some affect on the physical energy, it cannot prove the soul is saved. It depends on individual achievement.

Taoist knowledge holds that the soft body is one sign of the dead who has attained "untying the body." This person must clearly know before the time and make a complete preparation for his exuviation by finishing worldly obligations, etc. It is the achievement of self-cultivation. A teacher's help in opening the channel means some help. It depends on the teacher's energy as to whether he is truly helpful.

Q: Master Ni, since the point called the mystical pass is important, would you tell us more about it?

Master Ni: In the Taoist tradition, there are places in the body called the upper tan tien, middle tan tien and lower tan tien. The lower tan tien is where you refine your sexual energy, the middle tan tien is where you refine your mental energy and the upper tan tien, your spiritual energy. In India, they have similar points called chakras. There are some other terms, called the third eye or the heavenly eye.

This technique is taught, passed on by the technique of Taoist students. This knowledge or technique is called dien hsuan kwan, which means to open the mystical checkpoint. In reality, the mystical checkpoint is invisible in the human body; with spiritual achievement and quieting down, it will appear.

The point between the two eyebrows is what Taoists call the mystical pass. Some consider it a spiritual secret, but perhaps it is better to say it is a physical secret that at that point, one's individual spiritual energy connects with the body. The practice of touching or opening the mystical pass can be done by yourself by referring to the *Workbook for Spiritual Development*. Nobody can establish authority of doing that as an important secret held by an esoteric tradition. You can be helped by your teacher or spiritual friend. You also can be helped by yourself; that is the most convenient. Do not let anyone cheat you by saying they have any authority about this.

Chapter 6

Truth is One; the Teachings are Many

It is my goal to transmit the ancient spiritual development to all people regardless of their religious differences.
Yet, as a spiritual teacher, I first need to make my position
and viewpoint clear to you.

All general religious teachings were formed according to
a particular set of life circumstances. The circumstances of
those life conditions defined rules for moral and decent ways
to attain spiritual support or independence at that particular
time in history. That is how religious paths attempt to meet
or serve the cultural need.

In different times and in different regions, people were
looking for truth. They made attempts to try to present the
truth in a good way. Therefore, there are lots of religious
creations, right or wrong, that respond to the need for truth
with rules of moral and decent ways that give hope for getting
spiritual support. Those spiritual attempts later become
religions. They are not for us to insist on; in truth, they are
a supposition. All religion is, by its nature, expressed by
metaphor as an attempt by ancient sages to help people or
help themselves. We can appreciate that they made the best
attempt they could, but it is still not a place in which to stop
our progress.

After achieving themselves, people are aware of the
shortcomings or mistakes hidden in the books of the old
teachings. This is why all teachings must allow the new face
of life to come and make corrections and adjustments during
different times. Then more progress is made.

All general religious seekers are looking for spiritual
support, but few look for spiritual development. There are
two ways people learn to attain spiritual development. One
is indirect and one is direct. The indirect way is to first learn
an external religious teaching. Then, a person may come to
finally understand it and mentally put it in a suitable category
of life according to what kind of help he derives from it. Or a
person may reflect upon the teaching sufficiently to find out

it is not the ultimate truth, and start all over again to look for higher teaching to assist his spiritual independence.

In the past, many people followed an indirect religious path that used religious practices, but only a few people were not confused by them and became achieved sages. These sages gave up secondary religious doctrines to look internally for spiritual independence. At least, they might have achieved independence by not relying on the description of the spiritual world but by experiencing it themselves. However, few people travel on the indirect path and finally arrive at the direct teaching which is above religious forms.

The direct path teaches the student to be a spiritual person. What is a spiritual person? This question could be given several answers. One answer is that a spiritual person is a person who understands himself and the world enough to take complete responsibility for his actions, speech and thoughts. He no longer projects blame on others nor waits for someone to save him. Another answer is that a spiritual person is a person who has achieved a certain level of capability in handling himself in the world because he understands responsibility. Another answer is that a spiritual person is one who has learned to manage, control or maneuver his own energy.

There are also many ways to describe how one becomes a spiritual person. Few people go past the beginning stages, which include guarding oneself from the three poisons. The first poison is being aggressive and greedy, the second is holding hatred and bias and the third is attachment or insistence.

Human life is short. If one's goal is to attain spiritual development and become a spiritual person, it is not wise to lose time by spending one's entire life as a religious follower. Even if a person becomes a religious follower, it is not certain that he or she will derive enough inspiration to reach spiritual transcendence. Spiritual transcendence is being able to rise above the difficulties of working in the world; in other words, being able to maintain a positive spirit in all kinds of situations. As religious followers, people can spend their whole lives merely learning to rely on rituals and formalities. They become dependent upon those external things for their spiritual support rather than achieving themselves. However, it is possible that people can directly, without relying on any secondary doctrine, reach for spiritual truth. But if they give up when they have only gotten halfway, they might go back to the beginning and repeat the long process of indirect teachings.

I would like to give you an example of indirect teaching: in China, parents tell their rebellious children, "You have to be a good, obedient boy; otherwise, lightning will hit you." This is a kind of indirect teaching that uses a kind of threat. In some places, there are a lot of storms. People are sometimes hit by lightening and killed. Following Chinese custom, these people are not allowed to be formally buried in a tomb, because it is believed that they did something against heaven. The coffin is not allowed to be painted either.

Instead of giving a story, a mother would do better instead to tell her children the truth, explaining why they must obey the father and mother: because they are young and do not have enough experience to do the right thing. That is an example of direct teaching. The father and mother act out of love and protection to discipline their children. But parents so often do not tell their children the truth; instead, they make up a threatening story. It probably works to make the children behave, but the children become confused about reality. Also, it may leave them with a lot of unresolved, ungrounded fears.

Most religions teach fear in order to tame the undisciplined people of the world. In earlier times, the governments of most countries saw the function of religion as helping them to rule, and thus gave support to the religions. It was that type of governmental support that paved the way for the dominance of religion over society in history. It is not hard to find examples of this bad result. However, some people who are spiritually aware could see that the government and religion worked hand in hand. After seeing through this, still there were few people who could stay away from society. That was truly a bad condition of human life.

Even before people became intellectually developed, they did not find correct explanations for many things, and thus mythology developed. That is on a historical scale of a society. In a smaller scale, often a father and mother do not have all the answers for their children, so they tell stories. The indirect path of religious teaching is taught to people who have not yet developed an awareness of what religious practices actually mean. These people are spiritually undeveloped. They accept stories instead of developing the awareness of spiritual reality.

Another reason that indirect religious teaching is so widespread is that when people are children, philosophical explanations and spiritual truth are not easy to tell and so do not work to guide their behavior; metaphors and stories work better. Thus, religion created stories, but many people take those literal works as truth. Truth is difficult to communicate; that is why parents or religious teachers do not often say things directly. They are also aware of what the repercussions might be from speaking the truth. Their authoritative position of knowing the truth can be kept in the function of making others obey.

Once indirect teaching was established, it became a habit and a culture even if it lacked truth. For example, the religious tale of world order is something like a tree growing downward from the top. In other words, God comes first to develop downwardly from up above. In the human world, it is possible to first have the boss gather and make a crew of people as workers. However, you do not see that the boss was someone's employee before, and the reality is not that the boss comes to rule from the above; his business is a response to the need of society. The existence of business is commanded by the law of the relationship of supply and demand. Thus, from this illustration you can see that the correct order is from a vast foundation below.

In the natural world, nature is not started by a boss. At first, there is an authority. It developed through many stages by its own law. If we study or observe nature closely in many of its spheres, we will recognize that development does not happen from top to bottom. All things develop from the bottom and go upwards.

Even in spiritual teachings, a teacher is not necessarily greater than his developing student, because the student may reach and surpass his level of development. In this history of spiritual teachings, often we see that a teacher will reach a certain level of attainment, and his students will absorb his attainment and then take it further. Growth is not downward; growth comes upwards from the root. The teacher gives his teaching and the student grows up with it and may even achieve higher than the teacher. It is the student who made the progress.

Do you know the *Book of Golden Means* written by Tzu Shih, who is the grandson of Confucius? Tzu Shih developed his grandfather's wisdom and knowledge. However, Confucius' thoughts had not reached high maturity. Before his death, he even mentioned that, if given more years, he would study the *I Ching* further. It was not until his grandson, after persistent study of the *I Ching*, finally produced and wrote the *Book of Golden Means* which presents his own maturity based on the foundation of Confucius' expectation. It took three generations of hard work until his grandson, because Confucius' own son died early. Tzu Shih learned from Tseng Tzu, an outstanding student of Confucius. From this, you can see that no authority in the earlier stage of any field can be held throughout all the later stages. In any field or profession, although the predecessors achieved greatly, they can never be considered a final authority of the development of later stages. However, there was no more development in the Confucian school after Tzu Shih and Menfucius. Further advances in spiritual development occurred in new schools.

Although Menfucius was the last student of Confucius, he was the one who developed the Confucian school. The teacher and the disciple's life situations were different due to the different times that they lived in. Confucius traveled to all the small kingdoms, but he did not find himself welcome. Confucius was looking for a position in order to implement his idea while Menfucius worked to persuade the feudal lords in all the kingdoms he visited to stop warring with neighboring countries and to be kind in ruling. Although Menfucius was not successful in his efforts of promoting his peaceful goal, he was received as a friend and honored by the feudal lords. From the warm reception given to Menfucius, you know that the time and purpose was different.

One may think that without Confucius' work at the beginning, Menfucius might not have been welcomed and honored later. However, Menfucius was the first one in human history who served as a self-supported spiritual teacher and extended his teaching to all lords and kings. His teaching included individual spiritual cultivation. Regarding this, he was different from his teacher Confucius, who had put a lot of energy into promoting the dying old rituals, rites and social customs which were the lost civilization of earlier China.

Confucius had three thousand students, though only Tzu Shih and Menfucius could further develop Confucius' teaching. So attainment in learning, whether old or new, is precious in a certain stage until a new and better discovery replaces the old.

To stop development and growth is not the way of a true Taoist. One should not to be encouraged only to follow the old, but to grow further. In growing with the teaching of Tao, each student continues to attend to one's duty or responsibility in life while constantly looking for new opportunities for development and growth. A truly good spiritual teaching, as I view it, does not teach a tale of worldly progression as a tree growing from the top downwards. How could a world develop in that way? Such a teaching promotes the importance of rulership without giving the same importance to the ruled. This is untruthful. How can there be a political government without people. There is only God without the world and all ordinary lives. Without the common people, however, no ruler would be needed or produced. The teaching of the way of Integral Truth is not partial emphasis. It respects both; all the existence and the balance. A good spiritual teaching instructs in achieving balance in all aspects and levels of life, ranging from individual and societal to universal. A direct path inspires people to attain such balance.

The truth about attaining individual personal balance is an unchangeable truth. This truth is continually being refreshed and reproven. Balance is necessary for living a life of normalcy. For example, if an individual who lives in a family loses his balance, it will cause trouble for the entire family. The same is true in terms of society; loss of balance causes trouble.

There is truth in the earnest pursuit of living. The truth is in earnest life. When you search for your truth from the righteousness of living, then whatever you are, a mother, a daughter, a father, a son, a butcher or a physician, you have attained Tao. Whatever you are, do you live correctly, act correctly and practice earnestly? This is where the truth is seen. But some people place more importance upon the external facade of what their lives look like rather than the actual words and deeds, which is what their lives actually are.

Indirect religious teachings can only present the facade of internal truth through their pictures and stories. Religions do not pay attention to the inner growth of a person; they rush to look for external, artificial progress in their believers. Do you know the story of the farmer in the country of Sung? He saw his neighbor's crops growing taller than his own, so he went back to his field and pulled all the plants several inches higher. As a result, all his plants died. My point is that people need to grow correctly and strongly even if it is slow; if results are pushed without a solid foundation, then life is damaged. What each of us needs to look for is natural growth, not quick results. The processes of external religions or political parties is like industrial work that makes people like soldiers to follow external disciplines. Sometimes deep, real learning about life is slow, but that is preferable to going fast and missing the point or missing the depth.

If I have a spiritual standpoint of my own, it is different from what religions teach. It is an attitude of, let us grow together in the sense of helping each other. By this I mean, the way to grow naturally is to help each other. It is through helping other people that an individual learns and grows. This is not a new teaching; Taoist teaching has been recommending this for millenniums.

In China, there were hundreds or even thousands of folk religions, all indirect paths. Despite their efforts, not many people in Chinese society had reached the truth. When God has not been reached, the business of promoting God thrives. The leaders use conventional beliefs and names to back up their teachings, only to look for recognition for themselves which they transfer into self benefit and social expansion.

By the way: Nothing in teaching expresses anything new, although the leaders and the energy change. New teaching always repeats the old and adds other ideas. When this is used to crèate a new social force, it˙does not help people attain growth.

If we take a broad view of human spirituality, we understand that no one person or teacher can be an authority for all other people, because people learn from their own lives. People are all students. All people are students of each other if they are open to what is good and wise in other people. There might, however, be some who have learned more broadly and deeply. Such a person deserves respect, and should in turn work to teach and help others.

Some religious groups wish to take advantage of religious psychology and prey upon human fears. They create threats that encourage people to follow a specific dogma. Thus, people include immorality and sin, guilt or something to be repented in their religious structure. In the old type of society, justice or fair treatment was scarce. Thus, religion used concepts of heavenly justice to promote excessive emotions and to stimulate people's psychological life. People internalized those teachings and used their own emotions to regulate their behavior. Once you yourself can eliminate this need for oppressive emotions, even with external belief, the reliance upon external religion will become less strong. Working in this area, your own achievement is just undoing the trouble you have strongly held before but you can now see.

Although some threats can be a spiritual challenge, primarily threats are unnecessary in spiritual learning. The teaching of Tao does not use threats, it uses truth to help awaken people. This is why we call it the direct path.

The teaching of Tao instructs people to live a life of no separation from their spiritual nature. When people have fallen from their original organic nature of completeness and have forgotten what it was, how can they return to it? They cannot do it through stories, although stories may help them on a certain level for a while. They must do it through learning the direct truth of spiritual reality. In personal spiritual matters, a deeper understanding of self is necessary so people can find their way back to their own original nature. If people do not understand themselves, then it is hard to make internal progress.

My interpretation of original nature is this: a person's original spiritual nature is all bright and pure. This is why spiritual originality can also be called spiritual purity. After life experience or lifetimes of reincarnation, the reason the purity has been lost is not because the spiritual nature has been made twisted and contaminated, but because the mind is occupied by psychological problems. Thus, purity has been lost.

Learning how to regain purity is what the tradition of Tao teaches. My work as a teacher of this old tradition in modern times is to help each individual reach that originality and completeness, health and naturalness.

Let us go deeper into discussing spiritual originality. When a person reaches spiritual maturity, he has restored his spiritual originality. His psychological problems have been resolved. This is how I defined loss of purity above, but there is more to it than that. When a person reaches spiritual maturity, an interesting thing happens. At that point of maturity, there is really nothing that can be called spiritual maturity; in a sense, there is only the original being that is restored. Yet at the same time, the original being is a new being.

It is only by going through all types of life experiences that a person can reach spiritual maturity or spiritual originality. It sounds like a backwards trip, like a person is going back to something lost, but it is not, because a new spiritual originality is reached. The person is not the same as when he started by having taken lessons and remembering old ones. He integrates the understanding and learning from the new experiences and lessons into his personality.

That is why in the application of learning Tao, a mature person does not insist on returning where he was, the first spiritual originality, because he knows that he must reach something new. The new position, like the previous one, is also called originality because he does not stay there either.

New events and experiences in life are what make the new position an originality. Thus, maturity becomes a new original state of mind for all coming new events and experiences. One's spiritual originality will continue to grow and grow, because it is not a place where a person stays forever.

So when a person reaches a point of maturity or originality, he does not stay there forever; he keeps moving on to the next point of maturity or originality. Thus, originality is not something that can be counted or grasped. We are always moving toward converging points of new originality in preparation for our next step.

Thus, students of Tao learn differently than students of other spiritual schools. They learn the direct truth. In other schools, students learn something that keeps them in a holding pattern, either conceptually or spiritually. They learn the indirect truth.

Students of Tao are those who learn something to keep them going to face the vastness of the many facets of life and the profundity of internal spirit. Students learn to keep themselves going by learning the truth so they do not get discouraged about life.

Let us talk further about how spiritual learning goes from one person to another and how the valuable understanding of spiritual reality can go from one person to another. Material goods can be passed from one person to another, but growth and awareness cannot be given in the same way. How much of a teaching an individual understands depends upon his personal level of growth. A person's experience can be discussed, such as in a book or class. By discussion and learning, wise people are able to use others' experiences to help their own growth.

But books and classes are not needed at all stages of growth. How can a person start to grow spiritually? A direction of attaining spiritual growth can be set or a goal like expanding one's awareness can be known. Then, as a person keeps working in his chosen direction, he shall reach a place that is new to him. It is through reaching new places on one's way towards a goal that spiritual growth is attained. Spiritual growth can be received by continuing to learn through real life experiences, or even through psychological experience. The deepest attainment comes from real life.

Achievement from direct life experience is like highly refined steel which comes from a great heap of pig iron after undergoing a process of high heat. Personal spiritual achievement is the stage where the crude and coarse life being reaches the essential and non-descriptive reality of simplicity. Step by step, a person develops from a unattractive frog into a graceful white crane, from the ugly caterpillar into the beautiful butterfly. In other words, growth is not merely a conception. There is growth of mind in learning intellectually, but spiritual growth is different. Spiritual growth is a simple matter of development.

I have said on other occasions that each generation and society needs to attain its own growth and maturity. For example, on the scale of a society, China has a long history. She is old enough to be mature from the many kinds of experience that she has had. She should be wise; however, she is not. Why? Because the experience and wisdom attained from her experience is not continued from leader to leader or government to government. Thus, China remains undeveloped. If the leaders were wise, they would study and learn about the past successes and mistakes of their ancestors. Then they would begin to act by governing from the foundation of the knowledge they had obtained.

After forty years of wasteful experimentation in new social programs, the leader of the new generation did produce a bit of wisdom. It is: "It does not matter whether the cat is white or black; the point is whether she can catch mice." It sounded like the leader had finally awakened and broken away from the dogma of new ism. However, some time later, the same leader issued an order of slaughter for a group of students who were looking for conversation with the government. Have you ever heard of a country entitled "The People's Republic" that is so harshly ruled by the iron fist of its government and armed soldiers?

My point is that the only thing worthy of pursuit is for each individual, whether he is a governmental leader or not, to study and learn from our ancestors and from nature. In that way, each individual will attain growth and develop maturity, and be able to offer that to the world. This is true of both individuals and societies. Whether growth actually takes place is the difference between direct growth and indirect teachings.

One valid perception of my statement that the only thing worthy of pursuit is the necessity of moment by moment beingness. In truth, moment-to-moment awareness is a skill used in learning spiritual reality. Awareness is not the antithesis of growth; the two may appear to be opposites, but actually go hand in hand. Usually in spiritual growth, be it individual or of society, thesis and antithesis are linked together.

It is my understanding that the principle of Tao is harmonization of all useful differences and acceptance of all the colorful variety in the human world. Spiritually, harmonization and cooperation is the highest spiritual guidance of human people. It is above all religious divisions. Because it is universal spirit, it transfuses itself in all religions as their essence. Thus, Tao is the essence of all religions and is transformed into all the diverse religious expressions. However, universal spirit itself still remains transcendental and above the level of religious expression. This is why if you learn one of the religions, you still may not reach Tao if you have not reached the transcendental level. However, when you learn Tao, you have reached the essence of all religions.

Some religious leaders have tried to unify all faiths, but that is still not Tao. It only presents a combination of all religious teachings. Some religious teachers in history have made a good effort by combining all of the religions to avoiding fighting or conflict. But the teachings are still not the essence of the religion, which is the spirit. No one can adopt all the teachings because their presentations are so different; usually that type of combination only includes a few religions. But if a person exalts the importance of one thing, at the same time he forsakes the others.

For instance, Christianity teaches that Jesus is the messiah of the world, and Buddhism teaches that Maitreya is the Buddhist messiah. As they are different beliefs, you cannot unite them. Also, there is no need to destroy one or another.

In addition, some faiths encourage people to become serious vegetarians or to restrict one's sexual activity. Others take different approaches such as particular forms of exercise or singing. You do not need to reconcile those differences because they are not opposing differences. You can adopt any practical and helpful methods or behaviors into your own lifestyle.

If you deeply understand the reasons behind these practices, then you see the common strand they have that unite them. However, insistence on the surface cannot be reconciled. Yes, it is true, all religions have something in common, but limiting oneself to finding their similarity from the outside is only a mental task. We still need to find the divine energy that can work through us. In other words, what we need to do is find out what is inside; when we truthfully know what is inside us, then we understand all religions with no mental effort.

The teaching that is on the level that can be only spoken about is not the truth or the true path, but is a relative conception, just like all the schools of religious teaching. In teaching the truth or Tao, we use language to communicate. However, we stop short of the level of playing ideology. It has become the goal and the focus of our work to reach the non-relative truth through relative activity. In other words, the means we use is relative discussion, but relative discussion is not the end or goal. The purpose of spiritual learning is to break through any relative barrier formed as a confronting dual screen to reach Tao, the oneness.

Whether learning directly or indirectly, during a certain stage of growth, everyone goes through the conceptual level. Yet, a person can be good at conceptualizing and talking about things and still never be successful in spiritualizing his life. Understanding concepts is not the end goal. Those who do achieve themselves totally understand the meaning of the words and do not value the playing of words. Achieved ones are aware that it is relative conceptual habit that often causes further deviation from absolute truth.

So once they have understood, they integrate their understanding into the motion of their worldly life; in other words, they move into the realm of real beingness.

Thus, spiritual learning is different from intellectual learning. Some unachieved people are satisfied by the level of playing words. In truth, a person is not helped by staying on the surface and depending upon intelligence and general education. Spiritual development is related to one's own internal and external beingness. It is related to what you do with your life energy.

I would like to tell you about a great master. He was achieved, but you might not recognize him as such according to general religious custom. The life of this widely respected and recognized teacher can perhaps give you further understanding about the direct and indirect paths, the true and false spiritual teachings. This great master from the Sung dynasty was named Dtao Gi, but his nickname was the Mad Chi because his behavior, language and his way of giving help was unpredictable. People of conventional mind found him hard to manage. He performed many useful miracles. He spoke the direct truth and lived with the direct truth, yet he was a Confucian scholar and a poet. He became a Buddhist monk. He learned from his teacher and stayed in a Buddhist temple, but he ate dog meat, drank wine and went to prostitutes, things all expressly forbidden to religious Buddhists. He was freely open to all life circumstances that came by. He did all sorts of things. People who were overly serious thought that he violated all religious teaching, and considered him to be mad. If you judge him from the triviality of life without knowing that his spirit was freed from the world, you might think he was mad. Religious teachings set up certain standards to be spiritual truth and command people to live up to them, neglecting that it is the essence that should be embraced. It is not the trash or dregs. They over-emphasize that not eating meat or drinking wine is a big spiritual matter. Certainly these disciplines have value on a certain level; they are important personal issues on spiritual achievement. However, once you pass that level of worldly understanding, those things are merely the trivialities of life and not true spiritual essence.

Surely Master Dtao Gi was traceless. He was achieved spiritually by going beyond the forms of not only Buddhism, but also worldly life. That is how he was a great sage. Being a strict follower of Buddhism, folk Taoism or Confucianism is a level of achievement for some people, but a person of much higher achievement only follows spiritual nature. The Mad Chi was not a follower of any of the forms of religion. He did not need any formality to retain the essence. He could live freely, respond with people freely, heal people and perform feats of great spiritual power at any time. He totally liberated himself from any formality that anyone established as a religion. He was a true spiritual person of high achievement. He attained true freedom.

The achieved people look at their personal problems and personal worldly attachments differently than unachieved people. They are ready to face whatever with no fear. To be spiritual students, we need to learn to be receptive after having a better, deeper view about life matters. To nurture one's spiritual transcendence over all the matters of life is not merely a language.

However to a spiritually achieved one, such as Dtao Gi or another master, life is a group of conditions that meet together for no reason. It comes for no reason and goes for no reason. Actually, it is not that there is no reason. The reason is much deeper than your feeling. Nature becomes the prime reason for the lives. Once the conditions gather that form a life being, the form, its life, trouble and enjoyment can all be seen. Once one of the conditions fails, then the being scatters or disperses and goes back to emptiness. From emptiness came the birth of all. All is nature.

For example, yesterday you drove back from a nearby town. The road is not changeable, but the speed of driving is changeable according to the traffic, weather conditions, visibility, and so forth. Also, the speed limit changes at different points on the road. You make a change according to new information and conditions, but the truth of driving with good concentration does not change. There is no argument with that. What is true remains true. The truth is the truth. So Tao is changeable and also it is not changeable.

It is my understanding that Tao is the one road to truth. Many times I have been asked, "What is Tao?" Ancient teachers would not answer you. If I do not answer you, however, you will not learn. So in all different circumstances,

I respond differently to that question each time. Tao is not a dead thing. Tao is alive to be the most correct thing in all different circumstances. Or Tao is the opposite of all momentary changes. In this moment, if anyone asks me what is Tao, I would very practically answer that Tao is the most basic part of whatever exists. It is a road on which you travel. Or, it is a place in which you have reached, it is not the end. It is a road on which you can go further internally and externally. It is a road where spiritual nature meets physical nature. It is one nature anytime, because you have gone too far in one way.

Be open in approaching Tao. Do not hold onto your obstruction. Once a person practically attains Tao, he has achieved the breakthrough of his self obstructions. Liberation and freedom are attained by breaking through personal obstructions built over a long period of time. You might call them karma, but I would rather call them the obstructions or obstacles we have built for ourselves as protection or as part of one's unachieved being.

Personal previous knowledge - memory of past experience - can become a personal obstacle that prevent aliveness and awareness and correct response in a new situation. It is not only that personal knowledge can be an obstacle to progress, but so can insistence, personal limitations of growth, one's own health and one's mentality can all become obstacles.

If we wish to learn from Dtao Gi, our priority should be to learn his transcendental free spirit. Nothing could become an obstacle of your life, your spirit. Your light becomes so boundless. Then you attain true spiritual achievement.

People frequently talk about gaining the Tao. Sometimes people deceive themselves. People think that they know what gaining the Tao is; but what they think is truth is just words or a particular ritual; they have not learned the true spirit that is behind all words and can empower all rituals. They are learning an external form to fit a mold somebody set up for others. Therefore, if one is exceptionally proud of a form and insists that the form is Tao, he has misguided himself. Spiritual people cannot describe Tao with any form, shape or frame. Spiritual nature is high above any form. This is the true path.

From the example of the ancient achieved ones, to achieve Tao has not much to do with externals, forms, styles and regulations, but to attain the essence. You can learn Dtao Gi's liberated spirit, but it is not a good idea for you to learn his form or style. If you do, you will invite problems, because achievement is not something that can be imitated. It is something you reach by your own effort. A person does not need to express his achievement through "madness." While a person learns external religion, what he achieves is the forms, rituals rules, uniforms and wearing their emblem.

If a person worships Jesus or Buddha, he should learn the heart of Jesus or Buddha. If he wishes to learn from the Sixth Patriarch, Hui Neng, he should learn his essence but not necessarily his form. Master Dtao Gi himself, never in his entire sixty years of spiritual life, seriously tried to teach any formality. Instead, he always inspired people in different ways. This is a true model of free spirit. If you do not understand a sage's heart but you worship him, it is useless.

When we see the victims of those strong, confusing religions, we know that spiritual achievement by self-spiritual cultivation is of the utmost value. It is also valuable to relate to a truthful tradition in order to receive accurate teachings that will help one grow correctly.

What most people say, do and teach is not beyond the tangibility of a bubble. Like a bubble, all religious teachings are transient. Also, if anyone insists upon what Tao is, he fossilizes the living truth to be dead truth. Basically, the teaching of Tao is nothing that can be held because everything is in a state of change. The changing itself is Tao. If change is Tao, then which part of change can anyone call Tao?

If change is the truth, then what is called saving the soul by religions is actually losing the soul, because the soul is also not something always with the same reality. It changes, rising up and sinking down. What is saved is the original cause and poor soul. If a religion truly saves your soul for you, it damages your soul by taking away the opportunity to strengthen your soul, if you do not face your own challenges; you will not increase your own life strength. It is the soul.

You do not see that the lost soul will be gained and what is saved will be lost, because everything is changeable. To the religious groups, losing the soul is dissolving the self to join the natural spirituality, and saving the soul is to continue to be a ghost with a strong ego. If a person can truly understand this, then one has reached another shore.

As I see, although many kinds of spiritual teaching have been established, the most important is spiritual self-help. Without spiritual self-help and cooperation with people of the same goal, spiritual achievement hardly can be reached. The truth is clear that self-help and spiritual cooperation is the most important two elements of the direct path.

Now I would like to share some Taoist verses with you. I will sing a few to you as a happy conclusion to this meeting.

I.

Long ago, a spiritually achieved one vanished
by riding on a yellow crane.
Here is his empty monument.
The magnificent building, the pavilion of Yellow Crane,
stands here.
Once the yellow crane flew away,
it never turned back again.
For a thousand years, only the white clouds
floating and flying above this place
which has not changed.

II.

The mystical door and the high essence
are hard to obtain.
If you get the idea, you must forget the words.
A live bird will die if you seize it too strongly
by your palms.
All phenomena of life are cleverly comprehended
in one line:
Chrysanthemums bloom afresh in frost
after all the glamour of summer is gone.

III.

With my empty-hands, I hold a hoe.
Walking in my bare feet, I am riding on a buffalo.
Passing over a bridge, I see the bridge flow!

Beloved friend, in the first one, the truth is like the yellow crane. When you decide to catch it by looking at it with your eyes, it has already flown away.

In the second, the truth cannot be held. It can be seen at the last by the general intellectual mind. The seeing truth makes no great use. Spiritual achievement is to see the truth before its exhibition.

For the third, I would like to ask you a question. How can the bridge be flowing instead of the water?

Now, I have the fourth.

IV.

The ageless teacher sings:

Empty your mind.
Be truthful with your being.
Weaken your ambition.
Reinforce your essence.
Be desireless of what would be desired.
Be unsentimental over what is nature.
Look for the reality when you are at your wit's end.
Do not believe what anybody makes up.
Then, there is no more
*   to be done by a wise person like you.*

I forgot to add one sentence; that is to fill your belly. Let us have some tea now.

Chapter 7

Tao Speaks to You

Tonight I would like to talk about "zero doctrine." What does zero doctrine mean? The general understanding of the word zero is nothing, so from the words, "zero doctrine" you might almost believe that there is no doctrine. That is actually almost close to the teaching of Tao, because Tao does not emphasize any point of view. It is neutral like zero. It does not hold any particular standpoint which would create a prejudicial tendency. It rejects any possible extremes. Therefore, the zero doctrine is one way to understand or define what is Tao.

However, if we continue talking this way, then you will mistakenly believe that there is nothing to Tao and you will mistakenly believe that you are wasting your time by studying it and wishing to learn it. Actually, there is everything to Tao and it is the most important learning, no matter how you come to understand it. To help you understand, I need to further develop this point.

At the beginning, Tao just meant "the Way." Tao is the ancient spiritual education. It was especially emphasized about 2,500 years ago, when the wise people of society reacted to the confusion of the time. In order for them to help people, they took their wisdom and spiritual knowledge, which was an internal understanding, and put it into words or concepts so that they would be able to explain it to people. There were several different teachers, and as they taught, students came and schools were formed. At that time, the most popular school was Mo Tzu's school. It was the continued ancient Taoism. The way he worded his internal, intuitive understanding was to suggest to people that all people return to the faith of impartial Heaven by following the Heavenly Way. You must understand that he was talking about a good spiritual life, not a place with clouds or some impersonal and uncaring giant. He was talking about heeding one's own spiritual wisdom or internal energy awareness or conscience. He meant that one should be fair in every circumstance and not favor one person over another.

No individual human life should be emphasized above another.

Another school that was popular at that time was the Yang School. Some people categorize Yang Tzu's teachings as belonging to the Taoist school, but they are mistaken, because his teaching was quite different. Yang Tzu's philosophy is similar in attitude to hedonism, a teaching of ancient Greece. Yang Tzu emphasized that life is short and the mission of life is to enjoy oneself to the greatest extent. He believed that the enjoyment of a person is more important than anything else. By this theory, naturally the followers of Yang Tzu conduct their lives so that they enjoy much sensory excitement. They do not talk about what is truth and not truth, or about any responsibility or duty, tomorrow or yesterday. They talk about what they can physically enjoy now.

At the time, those teachings were popular. Even Confucius' last student, Menfucius, wrote that the majority of people seeking awakening considered themselves to be either Moist or Yangist. But Menfucius never mentioned the Taoist school in his writings, because he himself absorbed some teaching and practice from the ancient teaching of Tao. So you can see that the other achieved Taoists at that time still managed themselves with coolness and calmness: they stayed at the side and did not become involved with the changing waves of popular Chinese society.

However, Confucianism also developed its teachings. Confucianism came after the time of Mo and Yang. It wished to use regulations, customs, family systems and a system of monarchy to bring order to the society as was done in previous times. The students of Confucius were ambitious to reform society through rules.

Inevitably, these three schools argued a lot because their points of view were so very different. All of this disturbance and stimulation, finally aroused the aged Lao Tzu, an achieved Taoist. He responded to the challenge of the situation and wrote his book, the *Tao Teh Ching*. He gave it as a gift to an officer at a border checkpoint when he left the central society. The man appreciated Lao Tzu's teaching, so he gave the book to the officer and left the noisy society to look for peace and quiet. It is to say that Mo Tzu, Confucius, Lao Tzu and Chuang Tzu all presented the Integral Spirit with a different emphasis. All of them took the duty of awakening and harmonizing the people, but the approach was different. Thereby, the pure Taoism, different from the religious type of Taoism, took the duty of awakening people of spiritual differences to the subtle truth, Tao.

You are probably wondering how the teachings of these three schools give respect to zero doctrine. Well, if you read the *Tao Teh Ching* carefully - which I highly recommend - you will notice that at the beginning Lao Tzu mentions that the truth is nothing. He does not mean there is no truth. He means that truth is not-a-thing. Not only does he mention that at the beginning, but he repeats it all the way through the book. So the ultimate truth is not something that can be defined by a set of words. What is definable is an individual's personal view, temperament, quality of mind, education, feelings and sensations. All of those things come together to present an individual's understanding, concepts and definition of truth if he starts to talk about it. But that is still not the truth. In other words, if you are going to define the truth, your definition does not define the truth; it defines your viewpoint of the truth. The ultimate truth, as Tao, can never be defined.

I write my books to give viewpoints of many of the ancient developed ones. Why? I do it because I hope that after reading and understanding many different viewpoints of Tao from the achieved ones, you will come to understand what the words cannot define. Your understanding of Tao will not actually be a set of words. It will be deeper than words.

The beginning of the *Tao Teh Ching* points out the oneness and the unity of truth. The second chapter shows that everything has two sides and the two sides help each other. The third chapter continues to say that even if all things have two sides, it is still important to have a mature attitude. People still need to reach maturity from their intellectual or conceptual development, which can be endless.

So all the arguments between the three schools, or between any points of view, or set of words, are not necessary. They are only different viewpoints of the same undiscussible thing. In a sense, they are all true, but none of them are exactly true, because Tao can never really be defined. It is like trying to define lunch to a hungry person. You can talk about the ingredients and the colors, the temperatures of the food, etc, but his listening to a description of it is not the same as actually sitting down and eating it himself. So why do I spend a lot of time writing books to talk about it? To help stimulate your appetite for it. You see, it is so much better than an ordinary meal, if you do not whet your appetite for it, you might settle for something much less.

So a wise one does not argue about how he defines Tao because he knows that each person views things from the standpoint of age, sex, personal growth, experience, education, etc. These differences between people cannot be solved by argument. Arguments about Tao usually occur only about words, not about the underlying reality behind them.

Would you like to know how the stories have caused the misconceptions and the problems of the world? Some of you may wonder if I really follow Tao, because I have not stopped my teaching with words. It is true that the truth is indefinable, and that talking about it does not reach it. However, I am working to serve your life. Conceptual activity is part of our life. A healthy conceptual life is not assertive. A healthy conceptual life is not confused by its own creation. People can be misguided or poisoned by their own misconceptions. Most of the big world problems are caused by the conflict concerning student replaced: thinking and living differently. If a person's mind is not clear, if it is clouded by confusion caused by misunderstanding, he will not see Tao. My work is to help you clear your understanding so that you can see. A healthy conceptual life is a positive manifestation of Tao, with the qualities of being unassertive and impartial. People can be misguided or poisoned by their own misconceptions. In fact, most of the problems of the world are caused by someone not seeing things clearly.

All religions are old stories and past experiences put into literary production. All stories consist of the elements of time, people, a situation, events and so forth. Thus, stories are formed things and cannot be held as a cure for today's problems or as the everlasting truth. Stories are records of events in human history. In religion, they record events surrounding human spiritual attempts to answer their own questions according to the level of growth of the people involved. This cannot be held as new progress.

Basically, Tao is life. True teachers of Tao do not set up the truth. We learn, and therefore we teach, a healthy standard of conceptual life as guidance for life. This guidance that I am talking about now is called zero doctrine. The spiritual mission of a Taoist is not like that of other religions. Religions promote, argue, fight for and protect already established ideas, faiths, thoughts, philosophies, rituals and so forth. But those Taoists who emphasize the importance of healthy conceptual life instead focus on their good creations and also focus on the zero doctrine.

So far, I have not yet explained what the zero doctrine means. I will give an example of it so that you can understand. In almost every classroom, there is a blackboard. When a teacher teaches something, in order to help the student understand better, he sometimes needs to draw a diagram on the blackboard. Once the blackboard is all written over, what does he do? He wipes it clean to make it ready again for the next use. That is called zero doctrine. It means to return to stillness, purity, nothing or zero. Zero means a point between negative and positive. For example, when we drive a car, we can put it in neutral. When we put it in neutral, it is in the point of being able to go either in drive (forward) or in reverse. It is the empty balance point at which a clear decision can be made. When we teach zero doctrine, we mean to teach you to return to the point of clarity and keep your mind flexible. But if you have already put a doctrine there, it means your flexibility of mind is already given up. You are fixed to that doctrine rather than looking for progress or growth. That is where a person dies, if he sticks to it. If you have a flexible mind, you can correct your mind about a situation, renew your mind, develop your mind and find a new replacement idea or solution.

Tao cannot be defined by the differences between what is in front and what is in back. Nor is this the Taoist mind. A healthy Taoist attitude always comes back to a neutral point. For example, once we notice that we have thoughts or emotions towards a certain thing or person, once we have built any kind of attitude towards something, we always need to put them aside to come back to the zero point. We must always be waiting for change. A stiffened attitude will prevent change or improvement from happening; an attitude of neutral or zero will provide the flexibility to flow with a situation, however it occurs. We cannot hold an already formalized, established or stiffened impression, memory or record of an attitude that one has already established towards something. Those things prevent positive movement, growth or change.

In today's world, people follow and fight for something established by somebody else without even examining it first to see if it is something worth fighting for. For example, they will fight for a religion. However, they do not notice that general religion follows the creation of somebody's mind. On the other hand, a Taoist nurtures flexibility of mind. That is the difference between the two. The mission of the Taoist is provide teachings for one's fellow people so they will be able to come back to having a flexible mind. It is done with the intention of saving people and the world from continual contention, disturbance, turmoil, war, and trouble on a big or small scale. In a situation of contention, at least one side has lost its flexibility of mind. For this reason, this is why Taoism presents the zero doctrine. That is what Taoists promote. People who have this understanding must examine all the ancient creations, whether they are right or not, healthy or not. They are able to view things differently with their broad sense and openness. We wish that people who understand how to use the zero doctrine would apply it to their lives. We also wish that people who understand zero doctrine would examine all the ancient creations from the zero point of view to see if they are healthy or not.

For example, some rigid practitioners in Zen Buddhism, believe that speaking is against Tao, so they do not speak at all. But what they have forgotten is that if something is said rightly, it is also Tao. Although the ultimate truth is indescribable and inexpressible, we are the life of this ultimate truth. Therefore, there is also a right way to live and to speak. We just avoid any type of stubbornness, personal opinion and predecided judgment. We cannot even become stubborn or opinionated about the point that Tao is unspeakable.

There is contention and conflict among people on a big scale and small scale. The most meaningless trouble is caused by holding ready-made ideas. It happens if someone does not return to the zero point, or if someone does not know the value of the zero point. The truth of Tao is the zero point, the point where anything can be produced. It gives birth to all things. Do you catch this point, spiritually?

It is important for people to have kindness. People can learn from those who have kindness to restore their flexibility of mind. Do not learn from people who produce and hold toxins. Eventually the toxins attack their hearts. In the world, we see there are so many toxic minded people. But, few people can restore their fresh, alive, elastic mind. As students of the zero doctrine, we truly know the value of the elastic mind. You see, all life comes from no life. All ideas come from no idea. All religion comes from no religion. Everything started at the zero point.

I would like to give another example. Because I devote myself to work in the spiritual field, I will talk about that. There must be an object, goal and environment to produce any kind of spiritual teaching. I mean a teaching must be produced by the stimulation of the environment. In other words, certain environments produced certain teachings. Objects and goals are something the person react to the environment which is something outside a person affecting the person. A clear object must be produced by a clear understanding of the environment, then spiritual teaching is brought forth. Moses' teaching was produced by his specific environment. As for Jesus, his environment and society were different than those of Moses, so naturally he taught different-ly from Moses. Mohammed also had a different social background, so his teaching was also different.

Now, several thousand years later, all the sages have so many followers. Unfortunately, the followers fight over which teacher is best or right. Or they argue over the teaching. I believe as I mentioned, Moses, Jesus, Mohammed and Sakyamuni had the highly cherished spiritual and mental quality. This kind of quality of mind is so valuable; this is why they become leaders. They were able to teach something that many people could follow. If they came back to today's society, would they teach the same thing in the same way? With their good minds, they would need to reorganize and renew their teachings.

Because things in the world change, there is no reason to hold tightly onto any teaching or establishment that began 2,000 or 3,000 years ago. Only the helpful principles that were taught should be followed, because principles do not change. All good principles can merge together as one good unified principle that exists prior to any of the momentary teachings that were developed. It is Tao. A good example is any principle which is able to return to zero once it has done its job.

Yet, in the zero doctrine, there is no excitement. It is not thrilling, but it is really truthful. It is really healthy, like eating tofu or soy products.

However unexciting, this is my message. Maybe when you are tired of the excitement, you will understand. This is the focus, the effort, the concentration of the main point that I teach. I would like this never to be lost. Each person must still find his or her own balance point. The balance point is different from holding an opinion from one's personal collection of knowledge and information. To hold the balance point feels much different, much better, than it feels to hold an opinion. So no argument needs to be created.

Some people might also think that my teaching is conceptual. Yes, what I say is a conceptual description of something which does not need to be established as an argument. The zero doctrine has no rivalry. It is matchless, because you only can fight something that is there. You cannot fight something that is too enormous to see. The zero doctrine is peerless in fighting. This last sentence seems to say that the zero doctrine is good at fighting. Yes, it fights nothing.

Also, it is important that a Taoist has the awakening not to let the naturalness of his life being be pressed down by the creation of the mind. Thus, we need a healthy conceptual life with good content. This is why we work, talk, teach and make friends.

We talked about zero doctrine. I adopted the word "doctrine" from the religious system of Tao of later generations. It seems the word doctrine is strong enough to explain this position. A good mind needs good government. There are several types of governments of mind in the human realm. This may be new to you, but practically it is nothing new at all. We see it in everyday life.

In examining the government of an individual's life, it is necessary to give some classifications. The first is physical government. It is for those who only have physical interest and are limited to this level without knowing the spiritual reality of each individual life. This causes the spiritual being of the individual to become dismayed or disappointed, so this makes the life gathering of the composure of individual energy has no root. In other words, it is like "taking the air out of a person's balloon" - the person has no strength or interest in life. It is as most people view their life and death, like a candle. Once the candle is burned to the end, the flame, wick and wax are both finished.

The second classification is spiritual. Spiritually, each individual has two groups of different forces within each life being. One group is spiritual, one group is semi-spiritual or semi-physical. The upper, spiritual one is usually called or termed as Hun in the Taoist tradition. The other group, termed Po, tends to be more material. Because it only has material desire, sometimes we call it the animal spirits. The type of government that is established by an individual's mind depends on which one attains leadership. In general, most people are under control of the more physical spirits.

The spiritual energy in an individual understands life differently than the semi-spiritual, semi-physical energy does. Because of this different understanding, the spiritual culture of human people developed. Many different religions, correctly or incorrectly, express the way any individual's spiritual energy wishes to harmonize and balance the lower part so that they work well together. Unfortunately, general religion usually overdoes it and suppresses the physical partner. Suppression is not correct government for your individual life.

In my tradition, we understand what composes a life. Just as a big society is composed of individual people, as I mentioned before, each individual person is composed of two groups of tiny, very subtle, yet different kinds of essence: spiritual and semi spiritual. Through spiritual cultivation, these two essences become perceivable by the individual who knows they exist within him. This is another stage of growth. Once you have known this reality of life, the spiritual guidance you choose for your own life comes from your own spiritual growth and your own understanding of life;, then you can reach far. It is no longer the imbalanced or inconsiderate demand from one side of the two forces within him. Thus, we know that the general spiritual demand to become overly religious is not realistically grounded. Spiritual growth is something that has to come from oneself. If a religious practice tries to suppress, demand or regulate the other side of life, it is external pressure. External pressure does not allow a person to grow freely; his response is not his own growth. There is no realistic, grounded growth within the individual life.

A good government of mind leads the life towards the bright endless spiritual future with the harmony and support of the person's physical foundation. When a person's main soul receives life, it is sheltered with flesh. This life opportunity is a spiritual enterprise which engages in the creation of a new life, so that a new, higher stage of evolution can be reached. A good spiritual teaching has attained sufficient spiritual growth and knows the spiritual truth. A highly developed spiritual teaching knows the spiritual truth through the growth of its leaders. Internal harmony can bring about eternal life with the grounded conditions from each individual's cultivation.

We know the doctrine of tai chi, which is two equal but opposite energies work together to create something. We are now moving from the zero doctrine to the tai chi doctrine. By the way, if you do not like the word "doctrine," you can use the word "dharma," "principle," "knowledge," or any other word. Basically, it means the same thing, but it is not as direct as Tao. Tao is everything. Thus, Tao is self. Though it is not formable, it can be firm. It is not controllable, but it is constant and persistent. How it underlies the constant possible development of human life can be subtly observed through all generations.

With regard to zero doctrine, I would like to quote an illustration from the book written by Chuang Tzu. Usually his stories only have a few lines but they possess great meaning.

The indistinguishable one lived in the center of the universe. Its name is Hun Tun. Hun Tun received two visitors. One was the King of the East and the other was the King of the West. Hun Tun provided them all with his hospitality and showed them a good time. The King of the East and the King of the West greatly enjoyed themselves. They were happy and felt they needed to repay Hun Tun's kindness. On their second visit, the two kings brought their paint and paintbrushes. So they painted Hun Tun with nostrils, a mouth and everything that any ordinary life has. A new appearance of Hun Tun was seen, but then Hun Tun died.

Now, I will use Chuang Tzu's wording and repeat the story. Perhaps some of you may understand it better.

"The deity of the southern seas was called Shu, The One of Immediacy. The deity of the northern sea was called Hu, the One of Suddenness. The deity of the central zone was called Hun Tun, the One of Undifferentiation.

"Frequently, Shu and Hu met at the territory of Hun Tun, and for this generosity, wished to return the favor. They said, 'Every man has seven holes in his body for seeing, hearing, eating and breathing. Hun Tun is the only one without any, so we will drill some for him.'

"So every day they drilled one hole; but on the seventh day, Hun Tun died."

Beloved friend, do you understand what this metaphor means? The universal spiritual reality is not describable. It is above any human concept. However, all religions described it, paint it, drill it and make it look different and then hold that particular description as the truth of the universal spiritual reality. Thus, the universal spiritual reality becomes blocked by the words and the pictures of someone else's description.

In other words, people have been trying very hard to paint Hun Tun. Hun Tun is the undefinable truth. The leaders of religious activities try to paint the face of the truth. However, each of them paints Hun Tun differently, so a different Hun Tun is seen. Each attempt to paint or define Hun Tun makes him die. From this metaphor, we learn that if we would like Hun Tun to be alive, none of us should have the kind of ambition to paint Hun Tun the way we would like him to be. Let it be as it is. Some of you have seen Chinese opera. The personality trait of each character of the opera is portrayed by painting the actors' faces with different colored paint. Some characters are loyal, sneaky, cunning, straight, upright, beautiful, ugly, etc. Each character is painted with cosmetics, creating special patterns with different colors. So as you begin to watch a Chinese Opera, you already know what type of character the person is. It is similar to knowing who the good guy is in a TV western because he wears a white hat. But of course, when the performance is over, cosmetics and hats are removed, and the person's true face is seen. Now we don't see Hun Tun's real face, because the artistry of human achievement of the east and the west, in different races and tribes, tried to paint the face of Hun Tun, the indistinguishable truth. Similarly, if we were to remove the religious cosmetics, then the true face of Hun Tun would be seen.

Hun Tun, the undifferentiated oneness, is like an egg. Everything comes about from the metaphoric egg. A person can paint the surface of a thing, but he might still not see the internal reality of the thing. It is even harder to paint something that is alive, especially the internal reality of something, not to mention the subtle essence before it transforms into a thing. The spiritual reality of an individual has two kinds of different energies that confront and at the same time, assist and complete each other to bring about development. The harmony of these two spheres of different subtle energy we call the doctrine of tai chi.

The third doctrine is called the doctrine of nature. First there is nature with its spiritual reality behind it. Then we humans come along, experience nature, and seemingly having reached the universal spiritual reality, we use our minds to define or explain it. We insist upon how the truth of the universal spiritual reality is, or should be. But in reality, it should be as natural as it is without the interference of mind. Nature is life. Nature, in the practice of an individual life, means to give up or forget your attempt to manage all subtle elements, which support your life. Nature itself is a self enforcing law. Nature itself is not so shallow that we can manage all of it; the nature in people is continually an alternation of life and death. Nature itself is moving on a great path of evolution. Internally, its high essence keeps moving to push out the used remnants which become the material shell. This is the truth of nature, and it is also the truth of individual life. This good spiritual education was given by Lao Tzu from his learning.

We agree that Tao as the high universal reality is undefinable and indescribable. It is because the conceptual capability of the human mind is limited. If we use language to give a definition, the language and the definition automatically have the limitation of the perceiver's own view of what is perceived. Therefore, a learner of Tao does not try to define the great spiritual reality behind nature. It is Tao.

Yet, when studying the *Tao Teh Ching*, in many lines we can almost apply our conceptual development to understand what is Tao, the Way. In many other chapters, though, we can understand Tao philosophically and conceptually. It may give a subtle image of the imageless. However, through the identification of one's own spirit with Tao, one can be immediately united with the natural spiritual reality and have no more separation. Tao itself is not the substance of nature. It is not something like any other generally controllable substance. It is the potency. It is the insubstantial substance of the universe, as I am often forced to describe it in modern language.

Chapter 4 of the *Tao Teh Ching* says, Tao can be applied to the world. It means the principle of Tao. It is not forceful, yet it is so profound, as profound as the master behind everything. It also seems to be a power that mitigates the intensity of a worldly situation. At times you may feel the tension of your life to such an extent that you may feel as if the world will collapse. Practically, it is your own tension which is greater than the external pressure that is built among all people. Some would take it and push it to the verge of collapse. It seems that Tao is a kind of power that acts as spiritual calmness and peace to mitigate the intensity of a situation. By learning from the *Tao Teh Ching* to first lessen one's demands from life, one would attain the necessary inner power.

The same chapter also says that Tao is not only profound and difficult to reach, it also unties the entanglements, blunts the sharpness and softens the light, the shining blaze. Harmonizing oneself with the environment as the supportive essence in all environments is possible for those who know how to reach it. Those who are aware of what is going on around them learn to harmonize themselves with their environment and the world. They become a supportive essence in the decent environment they are in. Sometimes being supportive means leaving or doing nothing at all. When in an environment, you do not need to do anything, because Tao is the applicable awareness. We only subtly know the existence of Tao. We may not know where it comes from, yet it exists even before the first life. If we think the first being is nature or any divinity, we are mistaken; Tao is the mother of all.

In Chapter Six, Lao Tzu talks about the deathless essence of the universal valley. He is talking about universal vitality. This deathless vitality can be called the hidden essence. The gate of hidden essence is the root of heaven and earth. It insistently keeps producing lives and beings. From this chapter, we learn that yang is the phase from the subtle to apparent (expansion) while yin is the phase from the apparent to the hidden, latent, unmanifest vitality of nature (contraction). Here, we talk about the basic tendency of nature.

If we use the example of yang as spiritual, therefore invisible, while yin is material, therefore visible, the tai chi principle will fall into conceptual dualism. Dualism in metaphysics means the world is composed basically of two elements or two rulers. The tai chi principle as Lao Tzu is speaking of it here, however, is more like the theory of movement than talking about two objects. What is spiritual is yang, because it gives life and movement; it is in the phase of moving from the invisible to the visible. What is material is yin, because it is sinking and stagnant. It is in the phase of moving from the visible to the invisible. Yang and Yin are not two definite objects. They are two stages or two phases of movement of one thing or of one energy.

The tai chi principle is different from western metaphysical exploration. As philosophy, you have monism, dualism and pluralism. Monism means the universe is one element. Dualism means two elements and pluralism means many elements compose the universe. However, these thoughts are not the same as the tai chi principle. The tai chi principle describes one thing with multiple manifestations. In the stage of development, things and differences are displayed. Yet, when we reach the depth of energy, nothing is truly concrete or can be defined. Even a pair of opposites is interchangeable. Simply, it means A can change into B. B also can be changed into A. It is not definite, real, dead material as people view it; thus, we understand that the yin\yang theory or tai chi principle describes two phases of movement instead of two elements.

The tai chi principle can be exemplified by the earth receiving the light of the sun. The earth turns around by its own rotation. It is similar to roasting a chicken over a fire; each side of the chicken takes a turn in receiving the cooking force of the fire. So, with regards to the tai chi principle, the side facing the sun, light, heat or warmth, is yang. The opposite side which is far away from the sun, heat, warmth and light is yin. It is in darkness. The two forces of heat, or light, and cold, or darkness, continually exist. However, the part of the chicken in the heat or light changes. Thus, there is no rigid classification about what part of the chicken is yin or yang.

To divide material and spiritual as two phases of universal natural energy movement, what is spiritual tends to be the yang by its activeness and material is classified as yin by its stagnancy. With this key idea or basic standard in your mind, you now know how to classify all sorts of things.

The movement of the hidden sphere brings about the apparent sphere of lives and things. From this vitality, nature reveals its operation as the two sides of the tai chi.

Tao is the insubstantial substance. Most people's minds like to hold tangible things because it is easier to think about them. However although the existence of Tao is difficult to grasp, there is still some hint which gives us the possibility of reaching it. Chapter 14 says,

"Tao cannot be seen, heard or touched.
From these three natures,
    we know the nature of the universal spiritual reality.
Tao can be above, yet is not shining.
Tao can be under, yet is not dark.
You cannot see its head, nor can you see its tail.
However, it is the endless life of nature.
It is the endless source of our life."

Other chapters clearly describe the existence of Tao. It describes the non-existent existence of Tao, which can only be subtly understood and pursued and learned. Learn its gentleness, subtlety, selflessness, egolessness and non-competitiveness. Learn it does not live for itself. Learn it does not command or demand the establishment of itself. The overextending of oneself, like the beauty of the flower lasts for a short while, but finally it withers. When a person approaches Tao, because the energy changes, the qualities of gentleness, subtlety, selflessness, egolessness and non-competitiveness are naturally exhibited.

When we understand the delight of Tao, we understand that the game of human power, of wishing to have great influence over others, is childish because it is not a very interesting level of energy. Because the people on that level have not learned Tao, their overextension of themselves causes the essence of their life to become thin and dry out. There is one power, however, which brings new life. This power does not let anything overextend itself. It is the power of balance, the power of new opportunity and the power of the one who can reach the profundity of nature. Such a person can last forever, like Tao itself.

When you study the 25th chapter of the *Tao Teh Ching,* you will read that:

There is something that converges to be.
Before the birth of heaven and earth,
    It is a single and lonely, subtle life.
It is independent and makes no change in its reality,
    it keeps circling without exhaustion.
It can be the mother of heaven and earth.
No one knows its name.
Thus, we call it Tao.
We reluctantly describe it as great.
The greatness, however, keeps reaching very far.
But it still turns back.
Therefore, in the world, Tao is the greatest.
It gives birth to heaven and earth, and the people.
These three compose the universe.
The people abide by the earth.
Earth abides by heaven,
    heaven abides by Tao.
Tao abides by its own nature.

From this point, we suddenly understand. In today's enriched vocabulary, Tao is practically the universal soul or the soul of the universe. It is the source of the universe. It is different than the conception of God. God is to be. Tao is behind the "to be." Anything to be can change or cease to be. Only Tao, because it is not to be, remains as a potential to be or being able. It is a potence of the universe. God can only be one existence. Tao can be all the existence because Tao is behind any existence. Anything which exists can change or cease to exist. Only Tao, because it does not exist, remains as a potential for being or existence. God is an existence and Tao is all existence. It is like the relationship between a tree and its root, and a plant and its flowers. Thus, Tao is the potency the universe. Therefore, it can live forever. From this understanding, we finally find the root of life.

Now, we can come back to review the first chapter of the *Tao Teh Ching*. It says that the universal soul cannot be described, because it is not external existence. We can name it, but no name can completely describe it. So the "no name" is the beginning of the universe. Because it gives birth to all things, one possible name might be the mother of all things.

Conceptual ideas cannot reach its profundity, yet the conceptual mind can still subtly picture it. The union of the conceptual perception and the non-conceptual perception, bring the complete image of Tao. The two particular functions of mind can work together to reach the source because both come from the same source. The same source is hidden and profound. It is the doorway of all wonders.

In the second chapter, we know that at the stage of Tao or the universal soul, that is, the source of the universe, there is nothing that can be described as beautiful or ugly, good or bad, difficult or easy. This is because all is oneness and not split into the divisions of duality. In the secondary level, the hidden universal potency comes to the stage of existence where things seem contradictory to each other, that is, why the truth sounds paradoxical. For example, a person who takes the lowest position is in the highest, the weak is stronger than the strong, and there is a voice that makes no sound. Those two opposites which are a pair assist one another. One who develops his understanding of the subtle truth behind existence does not insist on describing things, because he knows that descriptions only contain partial truth. He lives by his true model, without making excuses from any natural obligation. He learns from Tao. Just like Tao, he is creative without taking credit for it. Just like Tao, he does not go to fullness and so does not become exhausted.

Chapter 3 and the other chapters all confirm the universal soul, the source of the universe. In order to make the book easier for you to understand, I have used the term insubstantial substance to describe Tao. It is also the soul of nature or nature as the single entity. Practically, one cannot deny the existence of the soul or nature, but it is not a substance.

Before we have talked about the doctrine of tai chi, we can relate it to the human world in terms of the two spiritual forces, Hun and Po. An individual whose Po is too strong is usually aggressive. If a person's Hun is too strong, the person is overly kind. Either way loses the center point or center middle way. Therefore, the principle of tai chi is the balance, or point of harmony, between the Hun and Po. An individual with balanced spiritual and physical energy is a useful and helpful person. If a person's Po is too strong, maybe he becomes a troublemaker without understanding the external situation or without consideration of other people's existence. If a person's Hun is too strong, he would be a withdrawing type of person who is not suitable for living in general society. He might find escape in some religious shelter.   Only the balanced people are the pillars of society.

Now, let us learn to unite ourselves with the universal soul, or the source of the universe. Chapter 67 of the *Tao Teh Ching* says:

> *Tao, the universal soul, is great,*
> *thus it is hardly like anything.*
> *If it can be controlled and, made exactly something,*
> *then it cannot be as truly great;*
> *It then becomes a petty something that can be managed*
> *by the human mind or hand.*
>
> *So the one who learns Tao, and unites himself*
> *with the universal soul*
> *expresses three virtues.*
> *The first is kindness.*
> *The second is efficiency.*
> *The third one is moderation,*
> *but does not compete for leadership*
> *in any circumstance.*

When we respond to a situation, if there is a need in an individual life which our internal essence can harmoniously fill, it is something worthwhile to accomplish. But once the mind no longer takes the lead, then there is a choice to go or not to go, to do or not to do, to take or not to take. At this point, we can grow with the opportunity. If we use our mind, we may just go in and try to help blindly. When our mind is empty, we can experience the choice point of to go or not to go, to take or not to take. We can flow with the energies of a situation and the opportunity instead of forcing or forging our idea onto it.   This is following your spiritual virtue, not following the impulse.

Now, we know there is a universal soul. The soul itself does not exist in the physical universe, while everything in the physical universe does exist as its being. The soul is united with the physical universe. The physical universe itself, with its myriad forms, changes, forms, unforms, conceives, and destroys in its operation of the entire sphere of life. However, everything in the material sphere has a time to come and to go. Only the Tao which is behind everything is always there. A life that is united with the universal soul never dies. It can continue to be. This life experiences the law of the tai chi with two spheres; that is, the two sides or the duality on the same level arise and compete with each other, within us and outside of us. However, it still embraces Tao. It means it participates in its life in oneness with Tao while still retaining its individuality. Thus, the life united with the universal soul experiences the duality of the tai chi sphere, yet still participates in the oneness of Tao.

The follower of Tao does not follow an external religion which organizes worship so that his energy is pulled outwardly into something. Tao is also not withdrawing and shrinking of one's being back to the center, but makes your senses extend to the depth of the root of life. In this way, you really plant your root deeply within the immortal realm. So the one who follows Tao is not an worshipper of the external. He knows the truth manifests in him or in her, once he lives a life exactly as Tao.

So, the normalcy of life, the decent way of living, is the main spiritual practice. It is the main spiritual ritual of the Taoist followers. There are still spiritual practices apart from the pure practice of daily life. These extra practices are only accessories; they are not the main practice. You are the book, you are the temple and you are the doctrine.

In other words, a good life itself is a doctrine. A good life itself is the external spiritual structure. A good life itself is the ritual of worshipping. Therefore, we have spiritual cultivation, which means to practice tai chi, eat a healthy diet and choose medicine which does not damage our healthy being, etc. This is all important in assisting and accomplishing the normalcy of life.

The constancy in life is the greatest learning of Tao. Tao is the constancy of the universe. Beings and things come and go. Tao is behind everything. It expresses its constancy as the root of everything. Its name is constant virtue. Tao is persistence; thus life is the persistence of the universal nature.

Individuals who live in the world are amazed by the attraction of material power, influence and pleasure. Such a person easily loses the connection with his soul. Any individual who cannot find his soul is lost. So each individual person needs to make the time to reach his own soul. The sages, the developed ones, have not only discovered and reached their own soul; they have found the universal soul. Although the soul of an individual is the essence of his physical life, in the background of the small soul is the universal soul which is the source of everlasting life. Tao is the common soul of all. The person who has found his soul will live in a balanced way. He will not live only for momentary pleasures, powers, fantasy, glories and mischief although he will certainly enjoy them if they happen to drop on his doorstep. He will live to find the universal soul. The one who finds the universal soul will have a life that is eternal, because he has deeply rooted himself in the eternal realm.

By deeply studying the *Tao Teh Ching*, no other religion needs to be learned separately. The secondary religious teachings tend to help others too much, which destroys the opportunity of reaching the truth in their lives. The secondary teaching as all religions, tend to shade off all challenges in life and thus destroying their opportunity to reach truth. It means they destroy the minds of people and make them unable to reach Tao, the universal spiritual reality, the common soul of all people and all gods.

Chapter 8

Who Does Better in Life
Is the Standard of Spiritual Truth

If we wish to evaluate a discussion to determine who is right and who is wrong from the standpoint of truth, first we must have an understanding of a discussion. This discussion is a good example of an argument between religious differences. It seems nobody really likes to discuss truth. What is talked about is mostly differences in the standard of truth, each person's impression of truth. It is really one's own psychological form but people mistake it for ultimate truth.

Someone asked me whether the truth could ever really be discussed by two people. This student thinks that everybody is so different mentally and in their lifestyles that it is really hard for people to agree on anything verbally. She thinks that on one level, the spiritual truth is the state of harmony or disagreement between people, the positive, negative, neutral energy or lack of energy flow between them, not the content of the words.

I will make an illustration of this point so that you will understand. In a child's hand is a cup of soapy water. In his mouth is a straw. He uses the straw to blow all sizes of bubbles from the soapy water. In each bubble is a reflection; sometimes there are twisted images of people, houses, landscapes and other things. When the child makes the bubbles, the other children at his side become excited about the bubbles and their reflections.

The real life discussion is not so different from children playing with bubbles, only the bubbles look different. There are bubble (Bible) worshippers. Sorry about my Chinese English, my pronunciation of the word bubble sounds like Bible. But is there much difference? Yes, it is the same. No, it is not the same. Bubble and Bible, how can they be the same? I know I am making a joke, but most religious believers are the worshippers of bubbles. The question is, what does a person hold as the truth in his life? Many people hold bubbles. Bubbles are interesting to look at, but it is not a good idea to base one's life upon them, because they pop.

They are interesting, but give nothing of real importance, except some fun for a while. There is nothing wrong with fun, unless one overdoes it. Let's keep our focus on a balanced, healthy life and not on just one small part of life.

In this moment, the students and friends of my tradition see the truth as holding the straw. Some people hold the bubbles as truth, and some hold the straw as truth. No one should neglect the child who is blowing the bubbles. That last statement sounds like an indication that the child is the truth. However, the child never thinks he is the truth. Soon he will become tired, begin to miss his mother, and run into the house, calling, "Mom! Mom!" The mother comes and satisfies his emotional longing. In that moment, the mother is the truth. The second moment, after being satisfied by seeing his mother, the child asks, "Where is my ice cream?" So then ice cream is his truth. You may not yet be clear how this illustrates the differences in the standard of truth. I will tell it to you clearly: On one level, the truth is what you need in different circumstances and stages of growth. The different standards of truth arise when people think that what they need is what somebody else needs, too. That is where argument arises and disharmony begins.

Many have read Lao Tzu's work. Lao Tzu says that the spiritually developed ones are not argumentative. People who like to argue are spiritually undeveloped. What does Lao Tzu mean? The problem is that it is hard to establish a unified standard of truth. If anyone found it possible to establish the standard of truth, then there would be no fighting or argument, and everything could be solved. This is a level of conceptual activity. The matters we talk about can be serious, but the nature of the talking itself is playing with bubbles. You play and play; just keep playing until one day you are tired of it and you stop playing. Then you go on to play something else; so a new standard of truth. In this case, the new, built-in standard of truth is that everything changes.

The worst thing in any argument, whether it is a friendly discussion or an uproar, is that each of us loses our sense of humor. Nobody is laughing, smiling or relaxed. The basic, naturally endowed capability of laughing is forgotten. People spend a lot of time discussing or arguing about something they think is important but which is really of less value than a simple smile or laughter. This "something" is the worldly religious tenets; they are nothing more than dust in one's eyes. If you call this a serious disharmony among human people or society, it is. Yet it is not the truth. The truth does not have any crisis happening to it. The crisis of disharmony happens to human people themselves; we forget to laugh. It seems hard for us to laugh. Perhaps it is not a good idea for me to recommend laughing in such a serious discussion as you might think this one is.

It's okay to play with bubbles if you recognize them for what they are and you do not take them too seriously.

People leave the arguments behind and go do something like T'ai Chi Movement or work for a charity or something because it is beneficial for themselves and others instead. That is a higher stage of spiritual development.

Let me use another illustration. Once a teacher was teaching in a place, and there were some children around the teacher. The adult students did not want the children to disturb the teacher and wished to take them away. But the teacher said, do not take them away; if anyone is like them, then he can enter my kingdom. He valued naivete in people because it is a positive and open attitude. It is better than being closed minded like someone who is fearful and pretends to know it all. However, children are only a small version of adults. They can be mischievous if there is no good discipline given to them or if their parents set a bad example through poor personal habits. Later, the teaching of this teacher became very developed. The fighting among his followers practically makes them a traitor to their teacher, who really preferred naivete. I am not talking about naive as ignorant and stupid, but naive as being open minded. Rather than being naive, people usually prefer to talk about what they think they know or understand, with an attitude of: "My understanding is truth. Your understanding is not truth."

When I lived in Taiwan, sometimes a team of two young people knocked on my door. They belonged to a Mormon church, and they politely taught me about the Mormon Jesus and the Book of Mormon. It is somewhat interesting, but it is not the promotion I enjoy. I enjoy the naivete or the good spiritedness that is behind the young minds. They came all the way from America to a foreign country to talk to people who conform to material benefit and short profit. They had never peered into the spiritual achievement of the true teachers. However, the naivete behind those young people is appreciable. When I was not too busy, I would let them talk and be satisfied. Then when they were satisfied because they had nothing to say any more, their true humanity would be shown by asking for water to drink or to use the toilet or changing the topic to real life.

Among the different believers of these religions, the mentality varies. Some are healthier than others. We see that beliefs can affect people's lives. Belief is an important matter, but it is clear what kind of faith needs to be promoted among people. Although we cannot stop people from playing with bubbles, let all of us appreciate and meet one another with our true personality rather than hide behind masks with different names. Once someone told me that the origin of the word "belief" was an Anglo Saxon word that meant "to wish." Each person wishes for something different; thus, each person's set of beliefs are different according to the spiritual growth of the person.

Small children are usually quite naive. The children who come along to a spiritual teacher are usually bigger children and not naive at all. When I was a child living in the country-side, we used mud to make all kinds of statues. Every child claimed that his statue was the biggest Buddha or the highest God. Finally some of the kids threw their statues at each other and started fighting. After children are finished growing physically, they learn to use their body to fight and so they create all kinds of reasons for fighting. Adults especially will use many reasons to fight each other. Religion is one of those reasons. So practically, to love fighting is their truth. They are not really fighting about religion or about the truth, they just love fighting. The subject matter of truth is only an excuse for the fight. I believe that children fight in imitation of the adult war.

In my tradition, we make spiritual integrity the model of spiritual cultivation. What does spiritual integrity mean? It means keeping your spirit intact; when someone insults you,

you find another way to deal with it rather than revenge. You use that "revenge" energy by transforming it into something that is more beneficial to yourself. Thus, you are the winner. The stage of babyhood is limited to the period of time when a baby still has red skin. Approximately, this is up to just before they can talk. During this time, they do not yet know how to fight. However, I am not establishing being as weak and vulnerable as a newborn as the way to live an adult life. We must be well rounded, with no more of those cutting angles that an un-unified adult usually has. Thus, no unnecessary friction is brought about and peace in the environment is supported. Truth is seen by a supple mind. The mind has not been tired out by intensified life experience. So many people lose the ability to be tender and gentle like a newborn. This is why I talk about it, to remind those people.

When Buddhism came to China, it brought a lot of new material to the Chinese people for them to talk about. The old books were too familiar; nobody learned anything from them because they thought they knew it all already. They did not understand that they had not learned anything yet, that they were still at the superficial level of storytelling, so the new religion gave the Chinese a chance to have more stories to tell. Unfortunately, even with the new version of the truth, they still did not go any deeper than the level of storytelling. We know that some people need to watch bubbles and they derive satisfaction from the stories. Some of the people who stay at that level become teachers of religion. At the same time, because people cannot totally give up the bubbles from some straw holders, they make the bubble their truth. Even many monks cannot give up seriously relying on bubbles; the others who achieve themselves as Zahn (Zen) masters become the straw holders. Then, they take the straw for truth, not the bubbles. That is the difference. Religious elaborations are like bubbles. The bubbles come from the straw holder, the child. But the truth is still far behind.

What, then, is the final truth? I have been in the United States for thirteen years. So far the differences between my students, the friends who enjoy my teaching and the other religious followers, is the differences between holding bubbles as truth and holding the straw as the truth. What's the difference? Both are material things; as Taoists, we are interested in energy. Being the person who holds the straw maybe has some power or social prestige, but so what, unless it is a place of good energy? A group of religious followers worships and adores the bubble that the leader makes. The straw holders still do not see what is behind the straw, behind the child, and so on and so on until the non-existent truth. Perhaps some of students or appreciators of my teaching in the Union of Tao and Man should change the name to be "The Club of Straw Holders." It means they are still holding onto something. Neither of these two groups can see the truth of the child that has a different stage of growth and demand. All different stages of demand have different expressions. None have reached the truth, so I have nothing to hold as the truth. We are speaking relatively. Maybe some day, you can all put yourselves together to reach the truth, like the example of the truly achieved one, reaching maturity, reaching the fruition of spiritual cultivation. Spiritual cultivation is like using a large amount of pig iron and refining it in the fire to produce a small quantity of really good steel. Although truth cannot be fixed, our own process of continual refinement must keep on in order to make our minds naive and receptive enough to reach the direct essence of all things and events. Do not think that today what you hold is the truth. Soon you will give it up when you attain another inch of growth.

Oftentimes, talking causes you to fall into the trap of logical trouble. Or you will have trouble in reasoning and fall into the pattern of relativity. But to be wholly is the entirety of being. Reaching the entirety of being means directly presenting the core of being, with its depth and width. When you try to put your experience of anything into language, you can only mention part of something, not the whole being. It is as if speech is linear, but events are spherical. How can something spherical be expressed by a line?

So my evaluation for this meeting is for people not to establish the standard of truth for anyone other than themselves. Also they should not hold firmly onto the standard of truth that they have reached for themselves, because it may change.

Now these people have used all these moments to establish "your" truth and "my" truth. Being in a hurry to set the conclusion is not the Way. The way is to keep going on to reach the truth by refining our thoughts, inspirations, reasoning and deductions, and giving up the attempt to form or shape the truth. Fortunately, truth has not shrunk away from you. Truth is everywhere. If a truth can be formed, it is the form that you produce from your mind. Imagine that the truth should be this way. Any formed truth comes from a person's imagination or idea that truth should be a certain way. True, it can be that way, but it can also be other ways.

In China, we found that discussions and arguments cannot go anywhere spiritually. Immortality is a science or an art which cannot be established by an argument or discussion. There are so many secrets; first you learn a little bit, then you discover a little bit more. Then you learn a little more, then discover a little bit more. There is not much to discuss. There are so many conditions necessary to create a good spiritual environment and position. It is simply to be, it is not to talk. We have talked away the immortality which exists in each good moment.

The first requirement of the practice is the awakening of the subconscious. You see, each time we do things, walking, talking and even while asleep, we are experiencing immortality. However, the subconscious continues like the flow of water. It always keeps flowing, on and on. Unity or peaceful mind, which means controlling the subconscious, is not something to write or talk about; it is something to achieve. It is the substantial elements you feel and know, it is the way of experiencing immortality. That is not an argument; it is realistic work. Somebody who can walk on a wire extended a great distance over a dangerous waterfall gives a great performance. Such a person needs concentration; he needs to control his conscious activity, and also prevent his subconsciousness from wandering. If the person walking on the wire has even one slight wandering of mind, he will fall. Staying or being at the level of religious worship may prevent a person from experiencing his life in each moment; it is a wandering of the mind. Therefore, the person experiences falling, scatteredness.

Once, in my youth, I was playing around by imitating a sleep walker walking off a cliff. My eyes were closed and I fell and rolled down the hill, all because of my inattention to the situation.

Some people practice sexual tantra. It means a man and woman sit together and plug in to be sexually contacted. If the man or the woman cannot control their subconscious activity, then the energy is not there to be able to practice tantra. So in all meditation and spiritual teaching, the fundamental demand is the simple practice of control, of training the subconscious activity. If it is uncontrolled, it brings scatteredness on a deep level. Do we achieve it correctly? What part of our subconscious is a normal organic condition, and what part can cause damage to one's mentality or spirituality? It all comes down to self-government or self-management. Much skill and practice are required to be able to do it. It is much deeper than doing general religious activities or watching bubbles, but it is so much more directly beneficial to all of us.

In human life, it seems that people would rather have a friend or group come together to play with bubbles. Playing bubbles brings no benefit. It is only one stage that makes a person understand better. If you are looking for something that really benefits your life, after you have experienced widely enough and deeply enough, you will become more serious at a different level without merely being an admirer of the bubbles. The bubbles have different sizes, different brands; by this I mean different religions. It is all conceptual activity.

The truth to someone wishing to reach it, is not the straw. The life of the child, the playful mood of the child, the health of the child, the universal being of the child are all not the truth. So first, in spiritual development, people are aware of the bubble, then they see the straw. Then they see that behind the straw is the child. If you see behind the child, the row of things in line behind the child, then you come to a deeper sphere, you shall see the energy. Energy converges from nothing to be something.

There is a song that goes like this:

> *"In my hand I hold the hoe.*
> *I am riding on my buffalo.*
> *Across the bridge I see the water.*
> *It is not the water that is flowing,*
> *but the bridge is flowing."*

Yale Creek, a small creek near where I live, has a bridge. Before the bridge was built, there was water flowing. If yesterday, a person stood on the bridge and looked at the creek, he would have seen the water flowing. Today, do we still see the person watching the creek? So people do not flow slower than the scenery. With the same reflection, the person, the buffalo, the bridge are all flowing faster, when the water still keeps flowing in the creek. I also mean, the creek will be alive forever, it is the nature of rivers to continue. Bridges last between 30 years and longer. Buffalo live 30 years. People live between about 50 and 120 years and longer. So the water does not change, but the other objects do. This has been the same for thousands of years. Therefore in the eyes of the sages it is not the water flowing. It is the bridge, or the buffalo rider, that flows much faster than the water.

So I did not have anything to offer you through this discussion, except to tell you that you will not find immortality by discussing religion. If you really have spiritual interest, go one step forward: manage your subconscious. That is your big job to do. Then you can manage your mouth and your thoughts. Then manage your energy and manage your soul. But do not be fooled: teaching inward withdrawal is not ultimate truth. Nor is teaching people to form social forces using the banners of religion for war or social improvement the ultimate truth. The truth is when the inside and outside meet each other. Where do they meet each other? It cannot truthfully be discussed. You must look for it by yourself.

Now, sit well, and do some meditation for a short while.

Each person has his own concepts or conceptual being. The normal conceptual flow hidden in each person's mind is one important institution of an individual. There are two possible kinds of conceptual activity that occur in a person. One is a normal flow of conceptual being. The other is the conceptual bubble of the person, which are the illusions a person holds about himself, worldly life or spiritual learning. The first one, the conceptual flow, is normal. The other is subnormal, or at least has the inclination of being unhealthy. The primary goal of my work is to help straighten the conceptual bubble of each individual who wishes to have a healthy life to change the illusions into clarity so that people can see things clearly and deal with reality. When I reach out in my work, I aim at the purification of the conceptual content of individuals and the entire human society. This purpose shows the value of my work. I use conceptual discussions to uplift people and help them to see reality.

Among scholars or intellectual people, spiritual learning begins at the level of concept. But the conceptual level is not the entire life being of each individual. Deeper than this level is the subconscious level. Do you know what the subconscious level is? Sometimes people talk to themselves. Perhaps occasionally, suddenly a word or short sentence comes out of a person's mouth. Even though one is not in conversation or responding to somebody, it is the subconscious activity that keeps going on. It is not direct thought, but a sort of background noise or static. It talks to you; it gives you clues about what your psychological reactions are to the events in your life.

Spiritual learning can start from the shallow level of conception, then come to the deeper level of the subconscious. Then, still deeper, one comes to the level of using symbolic language, movement, posture and ritual. These can cause, if correctly and affectively done, the response of the person's own spiritual being.

We have discussed on other occasions that each individual is a small model of nature. Big nature has mountains, rivers, flat land, high land, streams and big sky with lots of stars in different groups, some shining more than others. The human body is physically shaped and also has a geographical appearance. It has high and low places, ridges, valleys, crevices and other features of physicality. That is easily seen and understood. What is less apparent but still true, is that spiritually, a human being is also just like the sky with different star systems. Within our individual entity, there is a spiritual system of energy just like the star system in the sky. They are similar. The spiritual practice of my tradition is to use the symbolic vibrations, rituals and so forth, to request the response of each individual's spiritual energy within his own body. There are certain spiritual performances, like pictures or some types of rituals. Some people think that original Taoism worships the Big Dipper and the stars, but rather, it uses the analogy or understanding of the Big Dipper as symbolic communication to reach the internal spiritual system. It is not superstition or the worship of ignorant people; it is internal discovery and living the fullness of life.

Most people live experiencing their emotions, mind, thoughts, intellect and senses. All of these can describe a person's life, but they are not a complete description. It lacks completeness because the person does not have the direct participation of his spiritual system.

From the viewpoint of shallow observation, you may say that almost every spiritual tradition is the same. In today's world, publishing is so developed that religions and traditions are available to us, as spiritual students, to observe, learn and study. When we study them carefully, we find that those things are all one system applied to particular groups of people. You can discover through reading the published records of spiritual traditions, that all kinds of spiritual teaching are one system that is applied to the unachieved masses. The different forms have become customs of specific groups.

With a scientific, pragmatic approach I have investigated in depth each of the original spiritual practices of Taoism. There are practices on many levels. On the conceptual level, one may read and write books, but there are also good ways of discipline to help one's conceptual life. The subconscious is a totally different level and there are practices to control and improve it as well. On the spiritual level, there is no possibility for communication except through symbolic language, the vibration of certain rituals and so forth, which allows the response or reaction of each individual's naturally installed system.

Understanding is still external. Conceptual creation is still external projection. Practices serve your own life being. You must have correct understanding and receive the due achievement out of it. It is not to make you stay with anything, internal or external. It is to make you achieved, not to make you an expression of a special society. That would be too shallow. Another important difference needs to be carefully understood. Other religions may shape your life to serve the religion, but the tradition of Tao helps you to serve yourself and the world better with no intention of permanent worldly establishment.

We have talked about living the fullness of life. It cannot be done on the level of discussion. The level of discussion only connects many religions, philosophies and ideologies. Then it only serves or attracts the appreciation of the conceptual mind without deeply reaching the spiritual level. The spiritual level needs a different practice.

Our tradition is known for immortality. A person may talk forever about reaching his goal of walking ten yards, but until he has moved one small inch, he has not gotten any closer to his goal. Also, conceptual activity usually holds some kind of coloration; this means it is usually biased or based on a person's experiences, so it is not impartial nor does it see clearly. So even if a person becomes highly achieved on one level, for example, the conceptual level, he still does not cover all levels. Therefore the intellect is not total learning. It is not the total or complete being, it is only one part. Maybe a person does better, speaks better or writes better, but in reality he may not live better than anybody else.

I need to shift, to talk about the standard of truth. You see, when I teach I must give my opinion about many things. I view things differently because the traditional standard of truth, the viewpoint of this tradition, is different than others. We make the normalcy of life and nature as the standpoint of truth. Therefore, if anything is higher than the standard, a person will deviate from the basic fundamental center. It will cause conflict, disagreement or at least be irrelevant to the standard of truth of the Taoist tradition.

After reading many books and listening to many discussions, if a person still does not see the traditional standpoint of truth because, although the truth can be described to a certain extent, a description is not the experience of the truth. He needs to look for it and experience it in his life. Then he will know what we are talking about. What we describe is the standard of truth of human life in totality, not any one person's standard. Basically, it is still easy to know what is the standard of truth of Taoism. It is the substance of life which comes from non-formalizing natural vitality. We make the substance of life, in discussion, the basic standard of truth. So anybody who comes to me with a different attitude or background can discuss things with me. Some people deny the truth, disrespect it or overly beautify it with fantasy or fanciful thoughts. Usually this type of person will find disagreement with the fundamental standard of truth of original Taoism.

It was our discovery that the general essence of life is the standard of truth. Truth itself cannot be limited to anything. But a human can do some research and study, and make useful discussions. If we are very practical about it, we can derive benefit from using our energy and time to learn about the simple essence of life as the standard of truth. If such study is too lofty or distant from our lives, then we will not find the benefit in it. As pragmatic students of Tao, if something is not beneficial, then it is not in our interest to give up our truthful simple life being to fanciful thoughts, ideology or spiritual fantasy. Spiritual fantasies are only a form of coloration of reality, a kind of false hope. If you are a student of Tao, you learn to see clearly. You study the learning of Tao, the simple essence of life and the standpoint from which to continue to develop and evolve.

When a person first understands that this teaching is my way of putting the knowledge together under such a foundation or system, he realizes that there is no need for argument. I wish to use this occasion to explain this to you. Tao is one Tao. However, Tao has two sides like tai chi: one side is expressible and the other side is not expressible. But since Tao is also discussable and expressible, we communicate with each other and talk about the subject. We are not playing the bubble here; we are straightening up our conceptual being. Each day we will continually purify our conceptual content, because it is our concepts which help or harm us. This is the reality we carry in our teaching, learning, cultivation and development. It is a priority in our lives.

We have talked about the Taoist standard of truth. Now let us talk about the scope of Taoist spiritual cultivation, because all the things we talk about are connected. From the achievement of doing Taoist spiritual cultivation, the next measurement or evaluation is for the individual who does Taoist spiritual cultivation to apply it to himself. After one starts to do Taoist spiritual cultivation, one soon comes to the step of measuring or evaluating oneself frequently to see what areas one needs to work on or improve. The physical being includes such descriptions as tall, short, fat, thin, good looking or ordinary. All those things seem to be one's natural endowment and not much can be done to change it. A Taoist knows the importance of the physical being, so he improves the internal system of the organs and does his best to maintain his health and the normal function of the body. So with regards to his physical being, the goal and evolution in each individual's spiritual cultivation is health and normalcy.

The next thing we examine in ourselves is our mental being. With regards to the mental being, some people are smart and some are not. More important than being witty or intellectual is a person's will power, a sense of responsibility and honesty. This is all from the mental being of a person. Surely we need to cultivate our mental being to see which part is insufficient or lacking. For example, some people have more patience, but some lack patience altogether. If the latter is the case, the mental being is not complete, so there is something to work on and improve. Wisdom and love are all contained in our mental being.

After the level of physical being and mental being is the level of emotional being. When you examine your emotional being, you look to see if you are gloomy or cheerful, depressed or over-excited, etc. Usually one's emotional being or state is affected by a combination of one's environment, external stimulation and internal condition. In cultivation, we are looking for balanced emotions. This means, can you keep yourself steady most of the time, or return to steadiness quickly and without a fuss? Some people are so emotional they are like water flowing over a dam. A balanced emotional being is very important to individual life, so this is also the goal of spiritual cultivation.

The conceptual being of a person can be knowledgeable or not knowledgeable, open or narrow, prejudiced or kind. That is the measurement of one's conceptual being. To improve is to keep the mind and to do away with all the preconceptions of people, the world and your own life.

We also mentioned the subconscious being. Sometimes one will do something unconsciously, without good control of oneself. It is important to notice if you keep yourself quiet, or if you are mixed up. All those things connect with one's subconscious expression; subtly you can see it and feel it. To improve is to learn spiritual cultivation and meditation of complete concentration.

Then there is the health of the spiritual being. This means, are you enlightened or still spiritually living in the dark? Do you put yourself together spiritually or are you still scattered? Do you find spiritual truth or are you learning the spiritual, truthful teaching it offers to you? In all, do you attain your spiritual health? You might like to make your spirit endure to live in all situations, and so on.

So each individual life being is composed of many levels. There is still your intellectual being, your social being and your financial being, etc. If decent, all are worthy for you to take care of them.

There is your moral being. Each level is like one link of a chain. Each link of the chain reacts to the other links. In our spiritual cultivation, none of the levels should be neglected, because all of the levels affect your spirit.

We talk a lot about health in Taoist cultivation. We wish to make ourselves have a good physical being, healthy emotional being, straight and clear conceptual being and healthy subconscious being. Some of those things nobody else can know about but you, so you are the one who needs to do the self-improvement work. Also, subtly, you can learn to feel, be aware of and know more about your spirit. Developed people can see other people's auras, which is the light being, and see if they are dark or bright, red or other colors.

An individual life is composed of many levels. In our spiritual cultivation, it is not that we learn to measure other people; we learn to measure ourselves: am I perfect? Because I am not perfect, I have something I need to take care of. All of these need to be included in our spiritual cultivation. However, it is not necessary to be perfect first before we start spiritual learning. We are not trying to make people become like robots on an assembly line either, that is not what perfect means. What we are promoting is continual self improvement, each person working for his own personal balance. Each person working to be his own perfect self, not some external standard of perfect. A person who does that is a perfectly balanced person.

Rather than look for self improvement, many people look for spiritual fantasy. I describe spiritual fantasy as this: it is something that people can see or talk about, and it is on the conceptual level.   A student of Tao has to go beyond the talking to reach the reality. So the reality is different than the description.   We are not crazy about the descriptions of the high beings and the sages that were sent and so forth. The reality is, are you going to be your own sage and a sage for others?   That is the goal and the realization.   Spiritual cultivation is the way or process of realizing the goal.

Each level of a person's being has its standard. So we must use good understanding to measure ourselves and evaluate the conditions of what our beings are right now. Is my emotional being balanced?   Is my conceptual being untwisted and straight?   Is my physical being well and strong?

In all, my work is dedicated to the well being of all of your spheres of life and the world.

Chapter 9

Being Heaven and the Heavenly Beings

Q: Master Ni, would you speak more about what you have taught us about spiritual soberness and spiritual tipsiness?

Master Ni: Spiritual soberness is retaining the ability to be attentive to and correctly responsive to one's environment, while at the same time meeting the needs of one's higher life goals (having a safe, healthy life being and providing a supportive environment for one's spiritual practice and learning). This means, whenever one is at work, doing a good job; if at home, doing your share and keeping correct behavior; when in the marketplace, being attentive to accomplishing one's tasks and alert to possible mistakes.

Spiritual soberness is one of the spiritual goals I have talked about. It is a type of service to oneself and others. Spiritual traditions must agree that the path to Heaven is through service to others because the constancy of working correctly can be a mirror to show a person how he is doing. If he loses his soberness, he knows it immediately because he sees errors arise in his work.

It is nice when you begin to see success in your cultivation of spiritual soberness. There are fewer errors in work and daily life, you begin to learn how to handle the ones that do come up, and you feel good about yourself and your life. People respond to you differently; maybe some of them stop trying to avoid you so much because you have something to offer them. Also, some things bother you less or do not have the power over you that they did before. Your life has a greater feeling of richness, smoothness and positiveness to it. As you always say, your life begins to have a more heavenly quality to it.

I believe that spiritual soberness is a good goal for many people. It is nice to describe it, but it is better to know how to start to achieve it. A person will achieve it by wanting it more than anything else. He just says to himself, "I want things to go well and right in my life at all times and in all situations," and then he begins to apply himself to seeing that it happens. Not just one day, but he reminds himself of his goal every day. Surely, no one can live a totally trouble free life, but there is a certain point you reach where you know you are beginning to attain that goal of spiritual soberness and balance. Just do not give up, no matter what happens in your life.

Spiritual tipsiness perhaps is not as easy to understand as spiritual soberness.

Everybody in their life needs some enjoyment. There are different kinds of enjoyment or "drunken feelings" possible in earth life. There are those brought by drugs or alcohol, those brought by illusions or religions, those brought by emotions such as extreme happiness or sadness, those brought by ownership of material possessions or certain relationships, those brought by accomplishing moral actions, and those that are purely spiritual. Whatever good feeling we reach is a kind of tipsiness or drunkenness. All are a movement of energy, but the difference between them is what energy is moved, how the energy is moved and the amount of harm or harmlessness involved in moving it.

Spiritual tipsiness is the most excellent form of enjoyment because a person can do it and still maintain his soberness and harmlessness. That is, a person can still meet all his obligations and responsibilities; perhaps he even does better at them. Spiritual tipsiness is not harmful to others or oneself. However, it is important for a person to learn the self control and good lifestyle that is necessary to experience soberness and tipsiness at the same time if they want the full delight. Tipsiness alone is not enough. It is so much more wonderful to have one's life going well externally and also have the good feeling of spiritual tipsiness or contentment.

It is nice to describe spiritual tipsiness, but it is better to learn how to attain it in one's life. You always encourage us to learn it after a person has attained his spiritual soberness or at the same time. It is done through constantly practicing awareness of the point between the nipples or heart center during all kinds of situations. For many people it is most easily experienced in quiet, alone times, but practicing it at all times, when suitable to do so, brings more result. This type of concentration moves the energy out of the intellectual head into the heart and creates the pleasant feeling. It is when a person stops thinking. Having a quiet or unstressful life makes it easier to do, because a person's energy is already somewhat more contained within his body rather than scattered out in confused or unnecessary events.

Spiritual soberness is when a person applies his life energy to making the world better. It is a movement of energy from the person's being out to the world. Spiritual tipsiness is when a person brings the energy back into his body to replenish himself. That makes it possible for him to continue to be around, work with or serve other people in whatever way his life requires of him. It is the delightful movement of energy like the breath; in and out. When the two are balanced together, there is a perfection of being. I believe that a person who can attain both soberness and tipsiness at the same time is what they call the perfect person. That does not mean that all is perfect in his external life, but that he is perfectly balanced.

To be concise, spiritual tipsiness is applied to the following situation to ignore the errors of people who have wronged you, mistreated you and cheated you. It means to forgive people without even mentioning their mistake.   It means to give no thought or memory to people of inconsiderate behavior.   It means to be insensitive to or to ignore irritations,   provocations   and   meaningless   challenges. Furthermore, it is not to notice people's ill manners or improper use of words to talk to you or about you, etc.

In many occasions of my teaching and writing, I promote maintaining a clear mind or clarity of mind. On this occasion, I would like to talk about its opposite in answering your question.   As all of you know, truthfulness, exactness, precision, accuracy and being matter of fact, are so important for both spiritual intellectual learning and all general work. In spiritual learning, unfortunately, the worldly convention is that the general spiritual teachings are ambiguous and lack clarity.   People only repeat what people before them said, without knowing the source of such description. That type of situation is similar to this story. Once a man went from his rural home to go to town, and while he was there, he bought a fish. On the way home, he stopped to rest for a while under a tree, and so he hung the fish on one of the tree's limbs. Unintentionally, he fell asleep; he woke with a start, realized it was late and rushed off without taking the fish. It was not until he was already home that he remembered the fish. However, because some important household or business matters occupied his attention for several weeks, there was no chance for him to go back for the fish.

Later, on his next trip to the town, he overheard some people talking about a place outside their village where a new tree shrine was built, and where the tree god was efficacious and responsive. The tree was able to attract fish, so many people went over there to worship the tree and look for blessings. When he heard them talking, it stirred his curiosity, so later that day, he went over and to his amusement, it was the exact same tree he had hung the fish on! Many people were there, worshipping or admiring it. Finally, he took lots of energy to explain what happened that day he hung the fish there. All the people there laughed, and then everybody went on their way.

In many spiritual traditions or teachings, the minds of later generations have deliberated over something of a simple origin and then they have made a big story out of it. This is how teachings are spread without clarity. This is why I am the one who calls out for clarity in spiritual teaching and learning. It is important to cultivate one's spiritual clarity and mental clarity in spiritual learning.

However, on this occasion, I am not talking about shutting off clarity in spiritual learning, but rather about a kind of spiritual clarity that has a feeling to it similar to artificial drunkenness. However, I am not talking about the drunkenness of religious followers who have lost their clear vision because they are following something absurd or obscure. I am talking about the healthy, good use of spiritual tipsiness which can be cultivated after a person has achieved spiritual lucidity. I am talking about a person who clearly sees the nature of life and all different kinds of relationships. This is a person who can clearly understand the world's problems, but is still not discouraged; he has not lost warmth in worldly life. He does not give up having contact with all normal world relationship. He is not even intimidated by his contact with the harshness and cruelty of some people.

Once you take a long, long time and you have spiritual awakening in your sight, you have already attained the good knowledge about the world, life and people. Two possible attitudes of life might occur from that awakening. One, a person who is clear about the world, people and himself does not like the world or the people very much because they might be trouble makers to other people and himself. That kind of clear-mindedness will become the negative fruit of life unless the person learns more deeply. That kind of attitude is like distilled water, which is not as nutritious, as good natural water. So those people are like distilled water: they would not like to become dirty, pulled down or troubled by the world, so they keep themselves far away from it. They separate ti.emselves from people by their clear mindedness. However, by separating themselves from people, they miss the spiritual and nutritional value that they otherwise might have achieved. So that attitude more or less develops into self-care, self-love, self-respect, self-pride, self-interest or general selfishness. That kind of clearness has no spiritual value. Those people, after achievement of this kind of clear mind, will withdraw themselves to a narrow corner and close their mind. They are no longer open to anyone's problem.

The second kind of attitude from spiritual clarity is when a person also knows that the world and the people in it are all troublesome. A person knows that close relationships are mostly uninteresting, such as the relationship between father and mother, son and father, sister and brother, etc. Those relationships are sometimes false because people are so selfish and each one is involved in his own interests with nothing to share together. However, even after totally understanding that, this type of person does not hold any kind of wishful thinking, great expectation or anticipation of his relationships, yet he is still nice with them. He keeps the normalcy in the relationship by fulfilling his part without looking to see whether the other one has done her part or not. That is spiritual kindness that comes from lucidity of the mind. It is applied by a kind of spiritual tipsiness that was promoted by the ancient Taoists. In many paintings of the

ancient Taoists called immortals, you will notice that they are
holding a cup or pot of wine in their hand. But it is not wine
brewed by any earthen product. The wine is brewed of
wisdom; the wine drinking is the spiritual symbol of a kind of
blurred vision that can be applied to an unpleasant situation
in which a person is pushed, stung or made to feel uncomfortable. How can any person accept such a difficult situation? A person can accept it easily when he allows himself to
be in a mood or mind of drunkenness by the kindness he has
brewed up. It is a true kindness, not the play of shrewdness.
When most people have tolerance, it is usually because they
have asked for something, are waiting for a reward or are
expecting something to be returned back to them. So this
gives them tolerance. Taoist tolerance or patience, however,
does not come from waiting for material, emotional or mental
payment from a situation. That kind of tolerance or patience
requires an specially achieved psychological or emotional
power to create a self-transcendent atmosphere.

Let us say you are in an awkward situation, a place
where people do not like or respect you, or where people do
not give you support or help or whatever you need at that
time. In so great a difficulty, you may remain poised, not out
of numbness of feeling, but out of your clarity about the
nature of people.

Success and prosperity bring prestige, respect, gifts and
help. When you have money, the banks write you letters to
offer you a loan. But when you really need money, there is no
bank voluntarily offering a loan, because banking is a
business, it is not a help. Do you understand what the
example means? In the world, not everybody is greatly
successful; not everybody has great prestige or prosperity.
Social vanity and worldly heroism is what most people all
fight for and struggle for.

The spiritually achieved ones do not admire social vanity
or worldly heroism. They respect the normalcy of life. They
achieve to know the normalcy of life contains the highest
spiritual value. They might become successful and presti-
gious, but they do not move their focus away from the
normalcy of life. It is the main goal of their life. They are

willing to be normal people and to live a normal way, not something special.

I am not talking about normal in the sense that modern people or newspapers define it externally: A person 34 years old who owns a house, has a wife and two cars, 2.4 children or whatever the average is nowadays, a dog and three goldfish. This is a pretty picture painted by someone's mind and that is average, not normal. I am talking about normal in the sense of living one's life as it is. A person does not have to prove himself as better than the other people or able to do better than his parents, be the hero of the world, savior of the universe or even meet the newspaper definition of the average guy. I am talking about not living a fantasy, but living your life as it is. Life as it is, is sometimes boring, uncomfortable or tedious, with lots of work and unpleasant environments, situations or people. Right? Hasn't that been your experience at times? So, how do they handle living an ordinary, normal life among the harsh world? You sometimes need a special thing. To support one's being in the real world, some directly use alcohol or some drug, others turn to religious numbness, while some join a persecuting force to try to re-order or change the world. However, a Taoist uses an especially made wine he brews from his wisdom. To be able to allow the world to be harsh, people to be cruel and situations to push him, the effect of Taoist special wine might be the great virtuous fulfillment of forgiveness. He forgives the trouble, forgives the world, and forgives any people who wrong or mistreat him. Taoists do not call it forgiveness, however. Calling it forgiveness is a dualistic level and also makes one's ego too big; it puts the other people lower than you so that they need you to forgive their error. It might be called "A Taoist's self-made tipsiness." This tipsiness and blurry vision keeps him from seeing the mistakes of others and the harm or loss to himself. He does not know how another has wronged him or how they have mistreated him. It is not that he does not see into it; he simply decides that he does not care about the small losses. He knows but he does not care. There is something much more interesting going on, and he can afford to take the loss anyway because he has built up his strength. He is such a wise and kind dummy. He does not push hostility to the extreme.

However, in practical life, some people feel pain or agony because they are too serious about every small thing. Sometimes, a person cannot be too critical or too clear about the details. The application of clarity or clear mind still requires a person's better management to know the right circumstance in which to apply it. So when one's spiritual tipsiness is applied to the right spot, it can be lubricating, useful or helpful. At least it can make one's legs stronger; a person can stand stronger with it. All of this is to say that when you give people an easier time, it is also giving yourself an easier time.

We really know nothing. All knowledge activity is on the relative sphere. What is right as we defined is only relatively right. What we think is wrong is but relatively wrong. We really do not know the truth. We only know what is not truth, because all knowledge which can be established and recognized is in the relative sphere. Thus, how can anyone be assertive to declare he has reached the truth? The truth is no truth, because it transcends all knowledge that we know. You do not know, I do not know, and he does not know. That is the highest and the deepest we can know. If anybody says he knows, he does not know, because he knows only what he knows. Truthfully, the truth is still known to the unknown mind. We do not know, but we follow the truth until we do not follow the truth and run into problems.

Truth is not instinct either. It is just the natural truth of all life. It is not an establishment. It is nature, just like a fish does not know why or how it can swim.

We usually take scientific knowledge as most truthful and accurate. You have received a scientific education, at least in school. However, it is knowledge, but it cannot be certain that it is all scientific. No knowledge is permanent knowledge. We think that truthful knowledge must be permanent, that is not written. You can be sure however, that the scientific knowledge you learned is not because it has changed since you left school. Your parents and teachers wished to put your mind to learn all of them, but now it has all become out of date. Some might even think that the basics are invariable. But, as you know, they are a temporary standard which somebody set for the convenience of the moving forward for the further probe. Thus, in science, nothing can be permanent. There are accepted suppositions. They are a language that is a way to establish a communication or pass around such information.

Then it comes to the last type of knowledge; you may think that mathematical knowledge is the most truthful. If that is so, then 1 + 1 = 2 must always be the same. In the real world, however, numbers and mathematics are really the most superficial. For example, somebody's one thousand dollars does not mean the same as your one thousand. Your two brothers are not the equals of someone else's two brothers. Every day you drive to a city and travel the same mileage. The meaning is so different with the same mileage which you cover in the different time, etc.

My suggestion here is not to become judgmental or overly opinionated for the meaningless fight.

Nobody should think of himself as a nobody, or a somebody. You are nobody and somebody always at the same time. This level is not a place to establish your judgement. Reality has no emotional involvement. One would also open to a reality that we cannot really 'know' anything, and that understanding that you cannot really 'know' except in a conceptually relative sense is the beginning of self awakening.

Sometimes when I am talking about spiritual strength, I use the term spiritual sufficiency. The *Tao Teh Ching* calls it self-contentment from self-containment of natural life. The two concepts have the same meaning: a person who is strong spiritually and cannot be blown away like the wind or who does not collapse or panic in a difficult situation. An observer would say that such a person has self-confidence. That is mostly used as a general English word. If a person lacks confidence in himself, if he has no spiritual strength, he always feels like people are tramping on him, or that he is a nobody. He does not know that how he feels depends on how strong his spirit is, not even necessarily on external achievements that makes a person "somebody" in the eyes of the world. A person with spiritual self-confidence or containment does not feel tramped upon, even when in a "losing" situation.

On the spiritual level, we do not talk about confidence. Confidence is more of on a physical level. Both lack of self-confidence and overconfidence may be a source of trouble which invites mistakes.

Instead, to describe the spiritual level, we have used the words spiritual sufficiency or self containment. With spiritual sufficiency, you feel you are born by nature, are a part of nature and stay with nature. You feel that you lack nothing and that you are able to fulfill your own life. You are not longing for the types of achievement that other people have done, you are not looking only to be the same as other people. If you go looking for other people's achievements, you are like a duck who is trying to sing like a lark. You feel disappointed that you cannot sing like a lark, but you do not see that you swim better than he does. Once a person knows his nature, he will be inclined to follow or be his nature.

There are so many people living so close to each other in this crowded world. People push other people, and people also imitate other people. The result is that they each lose their nature. So in this answer, I am saying that a person needs to do his best to fulfill his own nature, and thus learn to enjoy himself. How do you refine your own nature? By staying with yourself until you experience it. Then you will learn to enjoy yourself.

If Taoists have any special feature, it is that they know how to enjoy themselves in a difficult situation. A person can do many things that can change into a job or a means of earning money. Money has two sides to it. Of course it is a means for sufficiency and convenience in your life, which is positive. But it also has a negative side: it requires hard work to make it, and once you have it, you have to protect it from thieves, inflation, taxes, swindles, fraud, and your own careless handling.

For example, let us say that you are a person who is good at making money. You must learn to manage it, to protect and use it wisely and beneficially. As years go by, you will experience physical changing and emotional changing. You will experience relationships changing and the world changing. All change must happen; however, your money cannot stop all the changing, can it? If you know this, at least you know that money is not the goal of life; it is not a correct standard to support. There is no spiritual growth in merely pursuing or accumulating money without a higher goal.

What, then is the goal of life? The goal of life is the normalcy of life. However, who can keep one's life all the same? There is a Taoist proverb that says, "Keep open to the world; at the same time, return to yourself." Is this possible? Yes; however, it is the play of the balancing point. It is wisdom of life management. As I know, most Taoists were farmers, scholars or other people who lived in any 'decent' walk of life. Some may question the word 'decent,' and ask, according to whom? Who sets the value of what is decent? walk of life. Is the decency of the people who lived during the middle ages the same of that of modern people? Do people of different times and places think that decency is the same thing? To most people, decency means what is socially agreeable. Is what is socially agreeable really decent? For example, in previous epochs, if you take someone's daughter as your wife, you needed to pay a dowry to her parents. Otherwise, it was not a respectable marriage. Is that decent?

In different societies, do people really know the decency of life or do they just follow the cultural mode and religious customs? I am not talking about compromising to what is socially agreeable, but what is important and spiritual, I am talking about the secondary level of life, usually what and when you do not have much freedom of a choice. I am not talking about the spiritual decency of all times, all societies and all people. I am talking about what is momentarily in your life. It is obviously not right to bend your spiritual nature to society. Also, it seems you are unable to bend society to you. Achieving your important goal is to follow the middle range which offers the highest flexibility in maneuvering but you still can confirm your life to the decency beyond time measurement. As the ancient sage taught, "In big things, one should not change one's virtue. On the small scale, flexibility is applicable." As to what is a big thing and small thing, can this be known by one's own moral knowledge?

So by decent, I mean honest labor, healthy handling of oneself and other. Is healthy handling the same as smart handling? As to the reality of the business world, my suggestion is to live with our solid peace of conscience, and not to undermine the peace of conscience by earning money through swindles, theft or fraud. So with regards to the ancient Taoists, most of them were farmers, scholars or people who lived in any 'decent' walk of life. Whatever social or financial position they lived with, they enjoyed.

There are lots of good Taoist poems, all expressing how they enjoyed themselves. Some activities like doing T'ai Chi Movement, Chi Kung (Chi Gong), calligraphy, making a poem or singing a song, etc., were not done to produce money. These things bring about happiness to the doer. Mostly we do it for self enjoyment and self amusement. If you do not do anything like the meditation of peaceful joy, you can still amuse yourself with the same mood which brews the meditation of peaceful joy.

Now, I have a big story to tell. Once a young Taoist went to New York to work and was ready to go back home to Los Angeles. He was returning to Los Angeles on the same airline that he took to New York. However, the person who made the airplane reservations did not tell him that there was a layover in Dallas on his return trip. Well, he got on the plane, sat in his seat, shut his eyes and blocked his ears and began to do his typical meditation of peaceful joy which can bring him into spiritual tipsiness. So he sat there, greatly enjoying himself. When the plane landed at the airport, the stewardess announced, "We have arrived." So he took his luggage and walked out into the airport. He went to the ticket counter, and because this fellow is related to me, he called my son to come pick him up at the airport. He waited there for a while, but nobody came. He called again, and the answer was that they had already sent someone to meet him.

However, after waiting a while longer, he began to get mad, so he went out to look for a taxi. He told the taxi driver, "Take me to Santa Monica." The taxi driver said, "No," and drove away. He felt rather strange that the taxi driver was so unfriendly, and wondered if they did not want to take some one of a non-white face. So he went back into the airport, decided to take a bus and began to look for information about which bus goes to Santa Monica. It was a busy terminal and there were many buses, so he began to try to figure it out. During his search, the stewardesses from the plane he was on came by and noticed that he was a lost boy. "What are you looking for?" they asked him. "I would like to take a bus so I can go home," he replied. "Where do you live?" they asked. "I live in Santa Monica," he answered. They told him, "This is not the right airport; you need to go back to take another plane." So four hours later, he arrived in Los Angeles.

When he was finally on the airplane back to Los Angeles, he thought it was impossible that such a thing could have happened. There was no sign that said "Welcome to Dallas." None of the people in the airport were wearing Texas cowboy hats, and nobody spoke with a Texas accent. How was it possible that it was Dallas? However, it was Dallas. He enjoyed his peaceful joy and the trip, but a person had better apply it in the right situation. I am not sure that this fellow made a very good example of how to use spiritual tipsiness.

Honestly, it was me. However, I only misapply my meditation once or twice in a lifetime, or several lifetimes. Forgive me for my bad example.

My main message is that in human life, sometimes you feel bitter with your husband, wife, children, parents or someone else. You cannot be too clear about how they have wronged you or how they treated you or if they do things you do not approve of. However, you should forget their errors. Spiritual tipsiness helps do that. Because family relationships are a natural relationship, it is hard to put them in a calculator. When you are dealing with matters regarding certain people, you had better keep a little bit spiritually tipsy. Human relationship is different from spiritual learning, scientific study or experiment or fulfilling one's job obligations, where great accuracy, exactness and precision are needed. Sometimes you need to take a different approach with relationships. I do not know what you call it in English, but in Chinese we have a special term called the deepest kindness as the thickest graciousness or Huen Ho. Huen Ho is like the process of making rice wine; before it is distilled, it is a little thicker and more nutritious. In all occasions of difficulty in life, you need to be like the wine before becoming distilled and made thin. Now comes the words to describe what the ancient Taoists valued: it is unadulterated originalness and unaffected purity. It is different from generally promoted social manners or the religiously commanded discipline and practice. Those are the imitations that are not truthful.

In spiritual learning, in one's personal spiritual achievement, it is necessary to learn the truth and reject the untruth. Take the essence to nurture your soul. Do not eat the dregs, because they have nothing with which to nurture your soul. Those dregs are feed for pigs. In China, we have all kinds of wine; some people use rice to make wine and others use peanuts, sweet potatoes or many kinds of fruit. Taking the essence is nutritious and tasteful, but the dregs are usually just fed to the pigs. This is the example. It is important because we learn how to nurture our mind, spirit and body. We need to take the essence but not the dregs.

About personal life condition, many people live in a condition of much luxury, with a high material standard. Other people cannot achieve that. There is no need to build up jealousy for those who are more fortunate. Those with greater material fortune work harder to achieve that or else it is their personal destiny. It is a temporary reward with no lasting value. It is one's interest and destiny. However, the real reward in life is the spiritual enjoyment that a person has, and that is not necessarily connected to one's material destiny. Spiritual enjoyment and spiritual achievement are like really good wine; there is no place where you can buy them. This high essence is something that you brew.

All things have their purpose according to how they are applied. For example, Oriental people think ginseng is a highly nutritious herb. This is truthful, but of course its usefulness depends on the situation to which it is applied. It is helpful, for example, to a mother who is delivering a baby and who loses lots of blood. On that occasion, when the mother keeps a piece of the ginseng root in her mouth at the right time and sucks on it, it will supply her with lots of strength and help to stop the bleeding. This is a right occasion to use ginseng. It is extra energy. Generally speaking, the energy we rely on for our everyday activity or for our basic health and longevity is not extra energy; it is our own energy, the energy that we produce ourselves through our healthy lifestyle of good air, nutritious food, proper exercise, balanced emotions and positive activity. Whatever kind of vitamins or minerals that come from the sun, water or food we eat, all need to be transformed or remade into energy by your own body. So the best high nutrition is produced by yourself. It is a process of transformation.

I would like to give an illustration of how we use or transform spiritual nutrition. For example, let us say that you read a book, attend a class or learn something from a teacher. You have heard or read about it, but still you need to transform what you read or heard to become useful and nutritious to your own life. There are lots of people who hear or read about good things, but they do not do anything with this information, so there has been no grounding or application of the wisdom received. So you are the one who basically produces the nutrition for yourself by applying what you have learned. It is you who also produces whatever you need to sustain yourself in your life.

A person materially makes money, buys food, cooks the food and eats the food. Almost everything that you take from outside requires some kind of system to extract and transform the nutrition to make it useful for your life. In Taoism, we use the illustration of wine-making to describe this transformation that occurs in our body. So learning Taoism is much different from learning general religious teaching. General religious teaching promotes spiritual obscurity and ambiguousness. Taoism promotes spiritual clarity and tipsiness at the same time.

The religious teachers will tell you that when you go to the world, you need to be like a snake or fox. A Taoist is totally the opposite of a snake or a fox. Spiritually, you have to attain high lucidity, but in worldly matters, you cannot be too picky, too critical or too judgmental. You can be judicious, but not judgmental. Put your life being into brewing to produce the essence for yourself, but not into the stage of already being the leftover dregs. We keep brewing to produce the new essence or new energy. Yet we do not exhaust all the systems of our life being. We enjoy all of what we have produced, but do not stop the function to take new material from producing new essence.

You need to understand the image of the eight immortals. They were together with all different kinds of people, enjoying themselves. They have lived in the world, but at the same time, they were not attached to the world. It means they live in it but they are not caged or entrapped by their achievement. They maintain their freedom to move through all different kinds of environments.

We really do not necessarily worship or honor a person who already lives in the mountains, is already high in heaven, or has already finished with all the trouble of worldly life. That is a dead example promoted by the worldly religions. That is not a good example to those who are still entrapped, still alive in the world. We make an example of people who still live in the world but are not entrapped by the world. This type of person can live in a relationship, but not be entrapped by his relationships. I am talking about all kinds of relationships, boy/girlfriend, business, government, social; any type of people relationship. That is what we value. The shiens are free and spiritual people who have achieved spiritual freedom. They are happy people. They are people who have not put a stop to enjoying their achieved spiritual happiness or spiritual freedom. Thus, they are called immortals. Being immortal is a spiritual learning.

Practically, this means that worldly life has a type of bondage or a molding pattern. Each society has its system. No person can avoid all kinds of convention or regulations and so forth. But the people who are achieved are not bothered by any of it. They comply with it, but are not inextricably tied to it. They respect it, but they do not worship it.

I deeply respect the examples of the ancient achieved ones. Most people admire the shiens because they think that the shiens have nothing to do but sit around and enjoy themselves. People sitting around is a kind of obstructive spiritual image that blocks the development of their admirers. The real shiens are the ones just like yourself, who have the courage to live in a world that seems not to make any big progress. But they are not intimidated; they are here to work any possible problem out.

A heavenly kingdom or spiritual paradise is not built in the air. A heavenly kingdom is not our imagination. What a spiritually achieved person does is to make himself, his own environment and his contacts less critical, picky and cruel, and more friendly and accepting. At the same time, he works to improve himself, his environment and his contacts so that there is less to criticize. All this is to make the world a real paradise. People who are unachieved would never find that type of heaven a beautiful paradise at all. They think it is too much work. Paradise, a heavenly kingdom, happens to those who are willing to achieve themselves in their lives and never be intimidated or discouraged by difficulty in life.

The world is every person's business. Each person's life can make improvement in the world. The hope of the world is not realized by a religion, it is accomplished through individual spiritual realization. That means no self cheating or no self deception. With clarity, we know where we go. Broad or uncritical acceptance smooths friction and conflicts that would otherwise happen in everyday life. Spiritual maturity brings about avoidance of small friction and conflicts. Everyone's spiritual health increases in the group when one person's spiritual health increases. Heaven is the practical spiritual achievement of one person; then his friends, environment and people he contacts are all benefitted by his growth. At least he is not the one who plays tricks or mistreats people.

Let heaven be with you, the world, all religions and all spiritual leaders. Let them look for clarity; clarity is clear knowledge about spiritual reality. Do not use false hope which has been misapplied psychologically by unscrupulous individuals to take advantage of undeveloped people. Let heaven be with the political leaders. Let heaven be with everyone.

In my books and teaching, I promote that all of you become good people. How do you apply those principles of being good in your daily life? There is a unique way. Before you are totally achieved, I believe you will be looking for understanding. By reading whatever I have taught, you can attain a general understanding. That is good enough. Those understandings will work automatically during specific occasions when you need them. You might like to give up your hostility, and give other people a break. You may ask me, but what about other people? I want them to give up their hostility. My answer is this: If we wish to be a Taoist, a person of unadorned truth, we have got to be a thorough Taoist. We cannot ask or demand such things of other people, we can only demand that we ourselves do them.

So how do we change ourselves? We do it situation by situation. Before doing something, we always ask ourselves, can we afford to do this action? We need to check out ourselves and our position first. Can we afford to have people mistreat, wrong, trick or cheat us? If we can afford it, we do it in a relaxed mood. Some very wise people look very foolish at times because it appears that the other person is cheating them. But perhaps in that instance, it is their kindness that is giving help to the other one.

For example, your friend wishes to borrow some money from you. In this case, you are in a good situation financially so loaning the money would be no problem. This person then mentions something you would like him to do for you as bait to make you decide to loan him the money. He is trying to make a psychological influence on you. So what can you do in response? Do you respond to the bait or respond to his need? You want to make the balanced, correct decision. You must look at the reality of whether in this instance, it is wise that you lend the money to the person. Does the friend have the ability and the integrity to pay you back? You might not even care about that and still wish to loan the money to help out your friend. But you would do that only if you can afford the loss if he does not pay you back. But whatever you decide, never base your decision on the friend offering to do the nice thing for you. That could be a social skill, or it could be that the person just knows what you like. Do not let people influence you, just learn to make your own decisions for your own good reasons.

When unfavorable things happen to a thorough person of truth, like someone does not pay back the money borrowed, then he is not upset or surprised because he had the foreknowledge that such a thing might occur. He expected it might possibly happen. Thus, he has the strength to deal with the situation. He does not avoid the unpleasant outcome. He does not escape it. He lets the thing happen because he knew it might be a possible outcome and he was willing to take that risk. So, he never comes back to complain about it.

If a person is only half achieved, he had better not take risks. Such risks are too much trouble or too painful for him. He pays a price but he does not get what he wanted. Mostly all spiritual teaching, if it is normal spiritual teaching, promotes people to do good and to be good. In judging a teaching, it is important to look at the teaching source. Do the teachers do good? All spiritual teachers take their teachings from the ancient spiritual knowledge, so you can judge their application of their teaching by how they live their lives. Surely, people can make mistakes. However, people can grow from their mistakes if the teaching and the learning material is right and reaches the truth. There is no guarantee that the people who teach chastity and purity with their words actually live that way or that they will do it exactly. They call sexual activity a sin, but in practical life, if you look at it, you might discover that whatever they teach becomes a suggestion for themselves to do it.

I mean, do not look at other people to see how they are doing. If you look at other people, you might become discouraged. Look at yourself. If you choose to be a good person, you do not need to look at or imitate other people. Just be what you are. We are so crowded today in city life, in school life and in society; people are everywhere. For example, if a person works for a company, he more or less influences other people. People imitate other people in their way of talking or treating people. How can you be a kind person, displaying your original nature in the midst of our commercial, highly structured society? You probably think that you cannot, but you can. If you want to know how to reach that goal, do the following: Stop and examine yourself; examine what part of your attitudes and reactions to things that are only imitations of your parents, brother, sister, fellow students or work colleagues. You may find that what you picked up from them is not the way you want to be.

Check it out. You are looking for your personal original nature. You might find that spiritual happiness, contentment and sufficiency comes from your own true nature; it does not come from imitation. For example, two people work in the same company. Whatever kind of car the first one buys, the second one buys the same kind or better. Whatever kind of lifestyle the first one has, the second one has to have the same kind or better. That is imitation and competition. That type of behavior never ends. Imitation and competition are not spiritual freedom. Whenever one person imitates another, maybe for one moment he thinks it is happiness, but that happiness is not his own standard or decision. It is somebody else's standard. For example, leather shoes are shiny and tai chi shoes are not. They have different functions. Buying shoes is not a matter of which is shiny or not, but depends on the use of the shoes. If you live or work in certain places, maybe there is a standard for dressing. If there is no standard, you would perhaps rather find something that suits you well, something that makes you feel really supported and happy. Often when a woman sees another woman decorate herself with cosmetics or jewelry, she goes to imitate it. It is a fashion, and she feels happy about it. But that happiness is short-lived. Do not let a social fashion become the truth of life.

I do not say there is a downfall of human morality. We are looking for the inner strength of life. We cannot worship the external standard of a colleague or a famous star all of the time. So, just do what you can do. Be what you really are. Correct the mistakes you have been making, straighten up the misunderstandings within yourself and with the people in your surroundings. Usually, external circumstances do not need to be straightened at all; if you try to straighten them, sometimes it just causes more trouble. So do not try to straighten things, but just be your real self. Do you really know your real self? You do not know, because your thoughts and emotions are already programmed by your society, family and cultural background. But there is a way that you can express your true self within the context of your society, family and cultural background. You need to look for the truth of nature.

I have mentioned that a duck does not need to envy the singing of a lark and wish to be like that. Nor does the lark need to learn to swim as well as the duck. They are different birds.

World progress, individual personal progress can be made by simple steps. Be truthful with yourself. Be a thorough student of Tao, the natural harmony. It is not a big secret. Just choose to live a grass roots standard of reality of life and emotion. Those who truly live with a real heart are not those who live with the psychology of false hope promoted by religions. Religions continue to feed the bubble which might easily pop or break. People have lots of illusions because their false culture and their religion with its false spiritual teachings all promote illusion. You feel good about the teaching of religious promotion for a while, but you never can reach it because the thing is not real; it is a bubble. Once you turn out to be an earnest being of nature, how happy you become. This is a simple thing that many knowledgeable people who know about religions do not know. Instead, they worship so many deities, so many gods to help them.

However, all of this is not my personal offering. It is all of the ancient achieved ones who have told us these things. They told us because we have deviated from the simple truth by the pull of external attraction for too long and too much. Once we courageously turn away from external attraction to rejoin our self, our spiritual nature, here we are, as complete as nature. Here we have reached, but do not stay, instead we move forward.

II

Q: Master Ni, we know that the word "Tao" means "the Way." What is the origin of that word?

Master Ni: Tao is an ancient culture. Correctly termed, Tao is ancient natural spiritual education. It was a spiritual development of the ancient wise ones. Because Tao was so reputed and respected, the later unspiritual leaders also used the word Tao in their teachings. So there came to be two kinds of things called Tao: the true Tao and the false Tao. Tao practically means the Way. Therefore, we can call those two things the true Way or the false way. It is similar to how money can buy things; there is true money and there is also counterfeit money. Counterfeit money is also used by some people. There are some people who dare to do such things.

Because I am a student and an admirer of the ancient developed ones, I am responsible for what I am promoting. If my students do not know the truthfulness of Tao, then they will be fooled by the false Tao. The benefit of learning the truth of Tao is that it does not harm you. Tao does not cost anything. It does not ask you to pay for it. However, the false teaching always has a motivation behind it. At least they will make you belong to something. The truth, though, does not belong to anyone; it makes you belong back to nature. It makes you belong back to yourself. That is the first thing to remember when somebody offers to teach you Tao. You have to understand the motivation or the truthfulness of the learning itself.

In this moment, with the purpose of avoiding confusion, I would like to tell you where the culture of the spiritual education of Tao came from. It is necessary to remember the book called the *Tao Teh Ching*. You also need to know the source or background of the *Tao Teh Ching*: its teachings come from the *I Ching*.

We all have some knowledge about the *I Ching*. There are 64 hexagrams. The first hexagram is called Heaven, the Creative Energy of Heaven or the Creative Energy of Nature. During the Zhou dynasty, the order of the hexagrams was changed to make Heaven as the first hexagram.

Before and after the Zhou dynasty, the great leaders of each epoch worked the previous version of the *I Ching* and each put something more in it to further develop the understanding of the *I Ching*. So you see that the original *I Ching* was not one version; there were at least three different versions. For example, the *I Ching* was initiated by Fu Shi. Then Shen Nung and then the Yellow Emperor worked it further. When it came to the Hsia Dynasty (2205-1766 B.C.), it was titled the "*Continuous Mountains*." When it came to Yin

Dynasty (1766-1123 B.C.), it was titled "*The Great Collection*" and when it came to Chou Dynasty (1122-249 B.C.), it was titled *Chou's Book of Changes*.

At the time when Fu Shi wrote it, the order of the *I Ching* was different; the first hexagram was not Heaven or Chien. It was K'un, the Receptive Energy of Nature. So the first chapter or first hexagram originally meant to be receptive. So the way of K'un or the Way of Being Receptive is the translation or interpretation of Tao, the Way.

First of all, the ancient spiritual vision did not think that people are masters of the world or of the universe. They knew that universal nature or the nature of the universe is the main strength, main force and main leadership of the entire world. For example, can we choose to be born or not be born? We cannot. Basically, we are in a receptive position. Also, humans have a time to come and a time to go. We have a time to prosper and a time to transfer to a more hidden stage. Thus, we see that there are cycles to universal nature.

To be a human is to learn to be wise. Learning to be wise is learning to be receptive to what happens in the cycles of life. And being wise is learning to cope with the external changing in a better way. So the K'un Tao, or Receptive Tao, means to be as receptive and accepting as a minister, a wife, a mother, a son and daughter or a citizen. This is the duty or the rule of all ordinary human people. For example, we can use these terms of minister, wife, etc, as an illustration. Though we can be creative in many circumstances to take care of the assigned work and to accomplish whatever comes to our hands, we are sometimes in a position in which we would choose not to be. Life itself is not what we choose or do not choose; we are only receptive to being formed and reformed.

So if you have interest, you can study the second hexagram in today's order of the book, K'un; then you will understand what Lao Tzu teaches and what the *Tao Teh Ching* teaches. That book originated before the Yellow Emperor.

What Confucius taught much later is lots of establishment. During his time, people had the ambition to be heaven; they wished to expand their ideas and impose them on other people, all with the ambition to influence and group others. That type of life is what we call being used by the natural impetus or natural impulse. It always keeps doing, but it has no eyes or vision to see the results of its actions, because the natural potency or natural impulse is also blind impulse. However, when a person is receptive, then he has grown the eyes or ability to see, to know and to choose correct action.

So the *Tao Teh Ching* appears to have some unusual teachings, but that is only because they are not easily understood. For example, the book says to keep yourself in a weak condition. Or it says to keep yourself in a soft position, like an old hen, a valley riverbed or ravine. People do not understand what the book means, so we can make an example of the moon to illustrate what it means.

The ancient type of life had more connection with nature. Nature has cycles. Nature is a cyclic movement. It takes on sections of cyclic curves and becomes a rhythmic movement. Surely we can say that when we experience the darkness of night, we know that we shall soon enjoy dawn and the brightness of the day. When we suffer from the bitterness of the winter cold, it means the warmth of spring will soon come. Nature always says that life will return.

I mentioned the example of the moon. When the new moon, shaped like an eyebrow, starts shining in the sky and we see it, we know that it will soon be returning to be a full moon. In seeing the fullness of the moon, we know its light will soon decline. When the waning of the moon comes, then it will soon turn into the dark part of the cycle. So each part lets us know that the next part is about to arrive.

So the main teaching of the *I Ching* is not to overstretch or overexpand yourself. Why does it teach that so repeatedly? Because once you expand yourself to your highest or fullest point, it means you will finish with that and move on to your lowest point. So therefore the teaching of the *Tao Teh Ching* is to remain weak, soft and not fully grown, like a ravine, a valley, a woman or a hen. It means, you always keep a position, keep in a certain stage of a cycle. In that stage, you make yourself have room for more growth.

When Fu Shi firstly decided that nature is a development, he divided all development into three stages. The first stage is as the beginning, the middle stage as the time of achievement or fulfillment and the third stage is as the overly used strength or whatever presents what is overly done. When the eight trigrams were developed into 64 hexagrams, six stages of division were brought about. Each hexagram is two sets of development, three stages each. When they are combined, the second and the fifth are where the balance is usually seen. The third and the sixth lines still express a situation of overly done or too much.

The general religious teaching is to go to heaven, to become rich or attain high prosperity. But once you attain that point, where will you go? In a cyclic expression, when a bow is fully stretched before shooting an arrow, it means that in the next stage it must shrink back. If overstretched, the bow may break. My friends perhaps will wonder: if you could keep the position of the other stage, then why can't you keep this position of fullness? You cannot because the developing force is external and internal. There is no way to keep the original point, at least not in personal growth.

So the teaching of the *Tao Teh Ching* comes from the hexagrams of the *Book of Changes*, especially the hexagram called K'un, which was the first hexagram in the original order.

So always remain young. A young person is usually weaker than a fully developed adult. For example, let us say that somebody has made one million dollars, and believes that he has already achieved his top performance. So he has no more to go. Let us say another person has made a hundred million; he does not make conclusions about it, because he still has lots of potential to go. This is similar to the story of a girl who was just given a cow. She got a bucket of milk from it, and put the bucket on her head to carry. She began to daydream about what she would do with the money from the sale of the milk. Immediately she could see the beautiful clothes on her body, and imagined that she was invited to a dancing party. She was admired by many people in the party, and so she walked and looked aside at them, turning her head ..... and so the bucket of milk on her head spilled onto the ground and her party was spoiled.

People who have reached spiritual depth and width are not easily exhausted. The *Tao Teh Ching* hints that when many people have become too strong or become too proud, they then push or force others. Those people are small people, or at least they are small containers. By this I mean, they are easily filled by whatever they attain and become proud. A little knowledge, and immediately they think, "I am the king. I am the king of kings." But they have become such bullies. Someone else would say, "I am the greatest teacher in the entire world. My teaching is useful all the time." But their teachings are limited, because they have limiting growth, no big growth.

In the *Tao Teh Ching*, there is not much establishment. It only reveals the truth we might like to comply with in order to attain more. Spiritual education teaches internal spiritual unification. Because one's life has so many elements outside and inside, spiritual unification is so important. Other words that describe it are spiritual unity. The first chapter of *Tao Teh Ching* as it is today, Heaven, shows spiritual unity. The second chapter of the *Tao Teh Ching* as it is today expresses the inter-assisting and inter-accomplishing opposite. The concluding, finishing part of the *Tao Teh Ching* teaches that the most important thing, learning, attainment, growth is a good, earnest life and gives instruction on how to attain it. The entire teaching of the *Tao Teh Ching* was based on the *I Ching*. It teaches that the fulfillment of natural virtue in good life by itself is the heavenly way.

The heavenly way means you balance your own life. You have to learn enough so that you have something to give. If you do not learn anything that you can do yourself, how can you have something to give? In today's time, people like to give, but they do not learn enough first before they start. In my teaching, every question that comes along, comes more and more to the point. This is unlike the beginning, when I first came to the west; people asked questions that were more troubled; they had suffered from the psychology of a certain living environment. I believe that once we learn the big principles from the *Tao Teh Ching*, in the small situations all the answers can be attained and put to use naturally.

The teaching in the *Tao Teh Ching* is not like any small religion that talks about being heaven. Each religion talks about heaven, but they are competitive because they would all like to be heaven. Rather than being heaven, they are expressing the untamed animal nature of human people themselves. Religions are disguised competitive forces for social influence. But the imagined God of their religions cannot last. What do I mean? Even God or gods that stretch their influence into the sphere of tai chi must experience the cycle of expansion and shrinking, rise and fall. There is no exception. All the competitive teachings have a chance to gather lots of people, a chance to fall, a chance to gather understanding and support for a time. But time changes and life changes. If you understand change, you are receptive. But all those teachings are so assertive and cannot fit the changing.

So you are students of Tao; learn to be receptive. From different changes, we remain our best as a new life, never worn out. Even at an old age, Lao Tzu declared, "I am not born yet, I am still in my mother's womb." But many people are going to be assertive even before they have reached their maturity. So then, the world trouble comes from competition between them. The competitors do not see that they shall be washed away by the changes.

The Taoists sit at the side of the ocean, and see one wave after another attacking the rocks of the shore. We say that yang energy, which is the natural potence or the natural impulsive force, is just like the waves. The waves come from the ocean, are formed by the ocean, and rush to the shore where they meet the rocks; create a big noise, whoosh, splash of water, crash, then the water goes away. The waves come, again and again.

Spiritual development comes from quiet observation, like the one who sits on the shore, watching the waves. Surely any person can play in the waves, riding on waves like the surfer. The one who does that will then experience the up and down, the standing up and falling in the water. You are young, so you enjoy it. But however, the natural cycle, the cyclical movement of nature must be explained. In nature, human history or in an ordinary human life, nothing can avoid the cyclical pattern of movement whether you are a believer of a religion or not. In front of the ultimate law of Tai Chi, such fantasy is of no use. No person should work to speed up the stages of the cyclical sections, but should instead slow down the natural speed of the cyclical spiral of fastness. One can only work for his spiritual development to transcend the cyclic nature of the earth plane.

The religions of the later generations talk about reincarnation and about saving the soul, all with no real affect. The *Tao Teh Ching* and the *I Ching* always tell us: Nature gives birth to life. Life shall ride the new cycle to come back again. This continues all the time. A tree falls; it dies. Then a new tree will grow. An island will burn to ashes, but all new life, animals, birds and vegetation will come back again. The seeds of human life are not seen as vegetation. Souls are the seeds of life of human people. When you are in physical life, maintain your subtle seeds of life well, so you will always have a chance to come back and live again.

General religion tends to take a section of the reality as the whole cycle. Thus, they look at the downward or ending part of the cycle of life as the whole thing. Students of Tao, however, keep their focus on the fact and knowledge of wholeness that whatever dies returns to live anew. Renewal of life is the knowledge of the students of Tao; they are not stuck by death. By this I mean, the life faith of students of Tao make death a small part of the eternal life. They nurture the force of continuous living; they remain young in spirit in all lives.

Conclusion

The Guidelines of a Taoist

A Taoist is a student of spiritual growth who has nurtured a high spiritual awareness and spiritual responsibility to himself and the public. He or she is a person who makes no excuses, but improves his or her personal spiritual condition and gives spiritual support to others who seek to do the same.

He or she is a person who spiritually disciplines himself or herself and avoids all unnecessary confrontations with people. He or she is a person who gives up aggressive force to his or her fellow people and develops his or her own spiritual tenacity. He or she is a person who knows how to live effectively, work effectively and manage his or her emotions healthily.

He or she is a careful student, who through spiritual progress can appreciate the work of the ancient achieved ones, notably Lao Tzu and Chuang Tzu and others. He or she is a careful student who is ready to actualize the truth of the natural organic being in his or her personal and public life.

He or she is a person who may be treated by others unfavorably in circumstances of conflict or competition in small worldly matters but who always treats others fairly in all circumstances. He or she is a person who discovers more valuable things to learn in the process of achieving himself or herself and has less to argue or to brag about in making progress.

He or she is a person who can organize his or her own energy of body, mind and spirit into a useful, serviceable channel instead of becoming scattered or wasting it. He or she is a person of Tao. A student of Tao needs no push from others. He or she is a person who actualizes from the impetus of his or her own life into an honest realization of spirit.

BOOKS IN ENGLISH BY MASTER NI

Quest of Soul - New Publication!
In Quest of Soul, Master Ni addresses many subjects relevant to understanding one's own soul, such as the religious concept of saving the soul, how to improve the quality of the personal soul, the high spiritual achievement of free soul, what happens spiritually at death and the universal soul. He guides the reader into deeper knowledge of oneself and inspires each individual to move forward to increase both one's own personal happiness and spiritual level. 152 pages. Stock No. BQUES Softcover, $11.95

Nurture Your Spirits - New Publication!
With truthful spiritual knowledge, you have better life attitudes that are more supportive to your existence. With truthful spiritual knowledge, nobody can cause you spiritual confusion. Where can you find such advantage? It would take a lifetime of development in a correct school, but such a school is not available. However, in this book, Master Ni breaks some spiritual prohibitions and presents the spiritual truth he has studied and proven. This truth may help you develop and nurture your own spirits, which are the truthful internal foundation of your life being. Taoism is educational; its purpose is not to group people and build social strength but to help each individual build one's own spiritual strength. 176 pages. Stock No. BNURT Softcover, $12.95

Internal Growth Through Tao - New Publication!
Material goods can be passed from one person to another, but growth and awareness cannot be given in the same way. Spiritual development is related to one's own internal and external beingness. Through books, discussion or classes, wise people are able to use others' experiences to kindle their own inner light to help their own growth and live a life of no separation from their own spiritual nature. In this book, Master Ni teaches the more subtle, much deeper sphere of the reality of life that is above the shallow sphere of external achievement. He also shows the confusion caused by some spiritual teachings and guides you in the direction of developing spiritually by growing internally. 208 pages. Stock No. BINTE Softcover, $13.95

Power of Natural Healing - New Publication!
Master Ni discusses the natural capability of self-healing in this book, which is healing physical trouble untreated by medication or external measure. He offers information and practices which can assist any treatment method currently being used by someone seeking health. He goes deeper to discuss methods of Taoist cultivation which promote a healthy life, including Taoist spiritual achievement, which brings about health and longevity. This book is not only suitable for a person seeking to improve one's health condition. Those who wish to live long and happy, and to understand more about living a natural healthy lifestyle, may be supported by the practice of Taoist energy cultivation. 230 pages. Stock No. BPOWE Softcover, $14.95

Essence of Universal Spirituality
In this volume, as an open-minded learner and achieved teacher of universal spirituality, Master Ni examines and discusses all levels and topics of religious and spiritual teaching to help you develop your own correct knowledge of the essence existing above the differences in religious practice. He reviews religious teachings with hope to benefit modern people. This book is to help readers to come to understand the ultimate truth and enjoy the achievement of all religions without becoming confused by them. 304 pages. Stock No. BESSE Softcover, $19.95

Guide to Inner Light
Modern life is controlled by city environments, cultural customs, religious teachings and politics that can all divert our attention away from our natural life being. As a result, we lose the perspective of viewing ourselves as natural completeness. This book reveals the development of ancient Taoist adepts. Drawing inspiration from their experience, modern people looking for the true source and meaning of life can find great teachings to direct and benefit them. The invaluable ancient Taoist development can teach us to reach the attainable spiritual truth and point the way to the Inner Light. Master Ni uses the ancient high accomplishments to make this book a useful resource. 192 pages. Stock No. BGUID. Softcover, $12.95

Stepping Stones for Spiritual Success
In Asia, the custom of foot binding was followed for almost a thousand years. In the West, people did not bind feet, but they bound their thoughts for a much longer period, some 1,500 to 1,700 years. Their mind and thinking became unnatural. Being unnatural expresses a state of confusion where people do not know what is right. Once they become natural again, they are clear and progress is great. Master Ni invites his readers to unbind their minds; in this volume, he has taken the best of the traditional teachings and put them into contemporary language to make them more relevant to our time, culture and lives. 160 pages. Stock No. BSTEP. Softcover, $12.95.

The Complete Works of Lao Tzu
Lao Tzu's Tao Teh Ching is one of the most widely translated and cherished works of literature in the world. It presents the core of Taoist philosophy. Lao Tzu's timeless wisdom provides a bridge to subtle spiritual truth and practical guidelines for harmonious and peaceful living. Master Ni includes what is believed to be the only English translation of the Hua Hu Ching, a later work of Lao Tzu which has been lost to the general public for a thousand years. 212 pages. Stock No. BCOMP. Softcover, $12.95

Order The Complete Works of Lao Tzu and the companion Tao Teh Ching Cassette Tapes for only $25.00. Stock No. ABTAO.

The Book of Changes and the Unchanging Truth
The first edition of this book was widely appreciated by its readers, who drew great spiritual benefit from it. They found the principles of the I Ching to be clearly explained

and useful to their lives, especially the commentaries. *The legendary classic I Ching is recognized as mankind's first written book of wisdom. Leaders and sages throughout history have consulted it as a trusted advisor to reveal appropriate action to be taken in any of life's circumstances. This volume also includes over 200 pages of of material on Taoist principles of natural energy cycles, instruction and commentaries. New, revised second edition, 669 pages. Stock No. BBOOK. Hardcover, $35.95*

The Story of Two Kingdoms
This volume is the metaphoric tale of the conflict between the Kingdoms of Light and Darkness. Through this unique story, Master Ni transmits the esoteric teachings of Taoism which have been carefully guarded secrets for over 5,000 years. This book is for those who are serious in their search and have devoted their lives to achieving high spiritual goals. 122 pages. Stock No. BSTOR. Hardcover, $14.95

The Way of Integral Life
This book can help build a bridge for those wishing to connect spiritual and intellectual development. It is most helpful for modern educated people. It includes practical and applicable suggestions for daily life, philosophical thought, esoteric insight and guidelines for those aspiring to give help and service to the world. This book helps you learn the wisdom of the ancient sages' achievement to assist the growth of your own wisdom and integrate it as your own new light and principles for balanced, reasonable living in worldly life. 320 pages. Softcover, $14.95, Stock No. BWAYS. Hardcover, $20.95, Stock No. BWAYH

Enlightenment: Mother of Spiritual Independence
The inspiring story and teachings of Master Hui Neng, the father of Zen Buddhism and Sixth Patriarch of the Buddhist tradition, highlight this volume. Hui Neng was a person of ordinary birth, intellectually unsophisticated, who achieved himself to become a spiritual leader. Master Ni includes enlivening commentaries and explanations of the principles outlined by this spiritual revolutionary. Having received the same training as all Zen Masters as one aspect of his training and spiritual achievement, Master Ni offers this teaching to guide his readers in their process of spiritual development. 264 pages. Softcover, $12.95, Stock No. BENLS. Hardcover, $18.95, Stock No. BENLH

Attaining Unlimited Life
The thought-provoking teachings of Chuang Tzu are presented in this volume. He was perhaps the greatest philosopher and master of Taoism and he laid the foundation for the Taoist school of thought. Without his work, people of later generations would hardly recognize the value of Lao Tzu's teaching in practical, everyday life. He touches the organic nature of human life more deeply and directly than that of other great teachers. This volume also includes questions by students and answers by Master Ni. 467 pages. Softcover, $18.95, Stock No. BATTS; Hardcover, $25.95, Stock No. BATTH

The Gentle Path of Spiritual Progress

This book offers a glimpse into the dialogues of a Taoist master and his students. In a relaxed, open manner, Master Ni, Hua-Ching explains to his students the fundamental practices that are the keys to experiencing enlightenment in everyday life. Many of the traditional secrets of Taoist training are revealed. His students also ask a surprising range of questions, and Master Ni's answers touch on contemporary psychology, finances, sexual advice, how to use the I Ching as well as the telling of some fascinating Taoist legends. Softcover, $12.95, Stock No. BGENT

Spiritual Messages from a Buffalo Rider, A Man of Tao

This is another important collection of Master Ni's service in his worldly trip, originally published as one half of The Gentle Path. He had the opportunity to meet people and answer their questions to help them gain the spiritual awareness that we live at the command of our animal nature. Our buffalo nature rides on us, whereas an achieved person rides the buffalo. In this book, Master Ni gives much helpful knowledge to those who are interested in improving their lives and deepening their cultivation so they too can develop beyond their mundane beings. Softcover, $12.95, Stock No. BSPIR

8,000 Years of Wisdom, Volume I and II

This two volume set contains a wealth of practical, down-to-earth advice given by Master Ni to his students over a five year period, 1979 to 1983. Drawing on his training in Traditional Chinese Medicine, Herbology, Acupuncture and other Taoist arts, Master Ni gives candid answers to students' questions on many topics ranging from dietary guidance to sex and pregnancy, meditation techniques and natural cures for common illnesses. Volume I includes dietary guidance; 236 pages; Stock No. BWIS1 Volume II includes sex and pregnancy guidance; 241 pages; Stock No. BWIS2. Softcover, Each Volume $12.95

The Uncharted Voyage Towards the Subtle Light

Spiritual life in the world today has become a confusing mixture of dying traditions and radical novelties. People who earnestly and sincerely seek something more than just a way to fit into the complexities of a modern structure that does not support true self-development often find themselves spiritually struggling. This book provides a profound understanding and insight into the underlying heart of all paths of spiritual growth, the subtle origin and the eternal truth of one universal life. 424 pages. Stock No. BUNCH. Softcover, $14.95

The Heavenly Way

A translation of the classic Tai Shan Kan Yin Pien (Straighten Your Way) and Yin Chia Wen (The Silent Way of Blessing). The treaties in this booklet are the main guidance for a mature and healthy life. The purpose of this booklet is to promote the recognition of truth, because only truth can teach the perpetual Heavenly Way by which one reconnects oneself with the divine nature. 41 pages. Stock No. BHEAV. Softcover, $2.95

Footsteps of the Mystical Child
This book poses and answers such questions as: What is a soul? What is wisdom? What is spiritual evolution? The answers to these and many other questions enable readers to open themselves to new realms of understanding and personal growth. There are also many true examples about people's internal and external struggles on the path of self-development and spiritual evolution. 166 pages. Stock No. BFOOT. Softcover, $9.95

Workbook for Spiritual Development
This book offers a practical, down-to-earth, hands-on approach for those who are devoted to the path of spiritual achievement. The reader will find diagrams showing fundamental hand positions to increase and channel one's spiritual energy, postures for sitting, standing and sleeping cultivation as well as postures for many Taoist invocations. The material in this workbook is drawn from the traditional teachings of Taoism and summarizes thousands of years of little known practices for spiritual development. An entire section is devoted to ancient invocations, another on natural celibacy and another on postures. In addition, Master Ni explains the basic attitudes and understandings that are the foundation for Taoist practices. 224 pages. Stock No. BWORK. Softcover, $12.95

Poster of Master Lu
Color poster of Master Lu, Tung Ping (shown on cover of workbook), for use with the workbook or in one's shrine. 16" x 22"; Stock No. PMLTP. $10.95

The Taoist Inner View of the Universe
This presentation of Taoist metaphysics provides guidance for one's own personal life transformation. Master Ni has given all the opportunity to know the vast achievement of the ancient unspoiled mind and its transpiercing vision. This book offers a glimpse of the inner world and immortal realm known to achieved Taoists and makes it understandable for students aspiring to a more complete life. 218 pages. Stock No. BTAOI. Softcover, $12.95

Tao, the Subtle Universal Law
Most people are unaware that their thoughts and behavior evoke responses from the invisible net of universal energy. The real meaning of Taoist self-discipline is to harmonize with universal law. To lead a good stable life is to be aware of the actual conjoining of the universal subtle law with every moment of our lives. This book presents the wisdom and practical methods that the ancient Chinese have successfully used for centuries to accomplish this. 165 pages. Stock No. TAOS. Softcover, $7.95

MATERIALS ON TAOIST HEALTH, ARTS AND SCIENCES

BOOKS

The Tao of Nutrition by Maoshing Ni, Ph.D., with Cathy McNease, B.S., M.H. - *Working from ancient Chinese medical classics and contemporary research, Dr. Maoshing Ni and Cathy McNease have compiled an indispensable guide to natural healing. This exceptional book shows the reader how to take control of one's health through one's eating habits. This volume contains 3 major sections: the first section deals with theories of Chinese nutrition and philosophy; the second describes over 100 common foods in detail, listing their energetic properties, therapeutic actions and individual remedies. The third section lists nutritional remedies for many common ailments. This book presents both a healing system and a disease prevention system which is flexible in adapting to every individual's needs. 214 pages. Stock No. BNUTR. Softcover, $14.95*

Chinese Vegetarian Delights by Lily Chuang
An extraordinary collection of recipes based on principles of traditional Chinese nutrition. Many recipes are therapeutically prepared with herbs. Diet has long been recognized as a key factor in health and longevity. For those who require restricted diets and those who choose an optimal diet, this cookbook is a rare treasure. Meat, sugar, diary products and fried foods are excluded. Produce, grains, tofu, eggs and seaweeds are imaginatively prepared. 104 pages. Stock No. BCHIV. Softcover, $7.95

Chinese Herbology Made Easy - by Maoshing Ni, Ph.D.
This text provides an overview of Oriental medical theory, in-depth descriptions of each herb category, with over 300 black and white photographs, extensive tables of individual herbs for easy reference, and an index of pharmaceutical and Pin-Yin names. The distillation of over-whelming material into essential elements enables one to focus efficiently and develop a clear understanding of Chinese herbology. This book is especially helpful for those studying for their California Acupuncture License. 202 pages. Stock No. BCHIH. Softcover, 14.95

Crane Style Chi Gong Book - By Daoshing Ni, Ph.D.
Chi Gong is a set of meditative exercises that was developed several thousand years ago by Taoists in China. It is now practiced for healing purposes, combining breathing techniques, body movements and mental imagery to guide the smooth flow of energy throughout the body. This book gives a more detailed account and study of Chi Gong than the videotape alone. It may be used with or without the videotape. Includes complete instructions and information on using Chi Gong exercise as a medical therapy. 55 pages. Stock No. BCRAN. Spiral bound $10.95

VIDEO TAPES

Physical Movement for Spiritual Learning: Dao-In Physical Art for a Long and Happy Life (VHS) - by Master Ni.
Dao-In is a series of typical Taoist movements which are traditionally used for physical energy conducting. These exercises were passed down from the ancient achieved Taoists and immortals. The ancients discovered that Dao-In exercises not only solved problems of stagnant energy, but also increased their health and lengthened their years. The exercises are also used as practical support for cultivation and the higher achievements of spiritual immortality. Master Ni, Hua-Ching, heir to the tradition of the achieved masters, is the first one who releases this important Taoist practice to the modern world in this 1 hour videotape. VHS $59.95

T'ai Chi Chuan: An Appreciation (VHS) - by Master Ni
Different styles of T'ai Chi Ch'uan as Movement have different purposes and accomplish different results. In this long awaited videotape, Master Ni, Hua-Ching presents three styles of T'ai Chi Movement handed down to him through generations of highly developed masters. They are the "Gentle Path," "Sky Journey," and "Infinite Expansion" styles of T'ai Chi Movement. The three styles are presented uninterrupted in this unique videotape and are set to music for observation and appreciation. VHS 30 minutes $49.95

Crane Style Chi Gong (VHS) - by Dr. Daoshing Ni, Ph.D.
Chi Gong is a set of meditative exercises developed several thousand years ago by ancient Taoists in China. It is now practiced for healing stubborn chronic diseases, strengthening the body to prevent disease and as a tool for further spiritual enlightenment. It combines breathing techniques, simple body movements, and mental imagery to guide the smooth flow of energy throughout the body. Chi gong is easy to learn for all ages. Correct and persistent practice will increase one's energy, relieve stress or tension, improve concentration and clarity, release emotional stress and restore general well-being. 2 hours Stock No. VCRAN. $65.95

Eight Treasures (VHS) - By Maoshing Ni, Ph.D.
These exercises help open blocks in a person's energy flow and strengthen one's vitality. It is a complete exercise combining physical stretching and toning and energy conducting movements coordinated with breathing. The Eight Treasures are an exercise unique to the Ni family. Patterned from nature, the 32 movements of the Eight Treasures are an excellent foundation for Tai Chi Chuan or martial arts. 1 hour and 45 minutes. Stock No. VEIGH. $49.95

Tai Chi Chuan I & II (VHS) - By Maoshing Ni, Ph.D.
This exercise integrates the flow of physical movement with that of integral energy in the Taoist style of "Harmony," similar to the long form of Yang-style Tai Chi Chuan. Tai Chi has been practiced for thousands of years to help both physical longevity and spiritual cultivation. 1 hour each. Each Video Tape $49.95. Order both for $90.00. Stock Nos: Part I, VTAI1; Part II, VTAI2; Set of two, VTAI3.

AUDIO CASSETTES

Invocations: Health and Longevity and Healing a Broken Heart - By Maoshing Ni, Ph.D.
This audio cassette guides the listener through a series of ancient invocations to channel and conduct one's own healing energy and vital force. "Thinking is louder than thunder." The mystical power by which all miracles are brought about is your sincere practice of this principle. 30 minutes. Stock No. AINVO. $5.95

Chi Gong for Stress Release - By Maoshing Ni, Ph.D.
This audio cassette guides you through simple, ancient breathing exercises that enable you to release day-to-day stress and tension that are such a common cause of illness today. 30 minutes. Stock No. ACHIS. $8.95

Chi Gong for Pain Management - By Maoshing Ni, Ph.D.
Using easy visualization and deep-breathing techniques that have been developed over thousands of years, this audio cassette offers methods for overcoming pain by invigorating your energy flow and unblocking obstructions that cause pain. 30 minutes. Stock No. ACHIP. $8.95

Tao Teh Ching Cassette Tapes
This classic work of Lao Tzu has been recorded in this two-cassette set that is a companion to the book translated by Master Ni. Professionally recorded and read by Robert Rudelson. 120 minutes. Stock No. ATAOT. $15.95

Order Master Ni's book, The Complete Works of Lao Tzu, and Tao Teh Ching Cassette Tapes for only $25.00. Stock No. ABTAO.

Many people write or call asking for information on how to set up study groups or centers in their own community. To respond to such requests, the Center for Taoist Arts in Atlanta, Georgia has offered to show others how they have set up their own center and discussion group. If you are interested, please contact Frank Gibson, The Center for Taoist Arts, PO Box 1389, Alpharetta, GA 30239-1389.

This list of Master Ni's books in English is ordered by date of publication for those readers who wish to follow the sequence of his Western teaching material in their learning of Tao.

1979:   *The Complete Works of Lao Tzu*
        The Taoist Inner View of the Universe
        Tao, the Subtle Universal Law
1981:   *The Heavenly Way*
1983:   *The Book of Changes and the Unchanging Truth*
        8,000 Years of Wisdom, I
        8,000 Years of Wisdom, II
1984:   *Workbook for Spiritual Development*
1985:   *The Uncharted Voyage Towards the Subtle Light*
1986:   *Footsteps of the Mystical Child*
1987:   *The Gentle Path of Spiritual Progress*
        Spiritual Messages from a Buffalo Rider, (originally
                part of *Gentle Path of Spiritual Progress*)
1989:   *The Way of Integral Life*
        Enlightenment: Mother of Spiritual Independence
        Attaining Unlimited Life
        The Story of Two Kingdoms
1990:   *Stepping Stones for Spiritual Success*
        Guide to Inner Light
        Essence of Universal Spirituality
1991:   *Internal Growth through Learning Tao*
        Nurture Your Spirits
        Quest of Soul
        Power of Natural Healing
        *Physical Movement for Spiritual Learning: Dao-In Taoist
                Physical Art for Long and Happy Life*

In addition, the forthcoming books will be compiled from his lecturing and teaching service:

Harmony is the Melody of Tao
Golden Message (by Daoshing and Maoshing Ni,
        based on the works of Master Ni, Hua-Ching)
Eternal Light
The Key to Good Fortune is Spiritual Improvement
*Physical Movement for Spiritual Learning: Gentle Path Tai
        Chi Movement*
*Physical Movement for Spiritual Learning: Sky Journey Tai
        Chi Movement*
*Physical Movement for Spiritual Learning: Infinite Expansion
        Tai Chi Movement*
*Physical Movement for Spiritual Learning: Cosmic Tour
        Tai Chi Movement*

How To Order

Complete this form and mail it to: **Union of Tao and Man,**
117 Stonehaven Way, Los Angeles, CA 90049 (213)-472-9970

Name: _____

Address: _____

City: _____ State: _____ Zip: _____

Phone - Daytime: _____ Evening: _____

(We may telephone you if we have questions about your order.)

Qty.	Stock No.	Title/Description	Price Each	Total Price

Total amount for items ordered_____

Sales tax (CA residents, 6-1/2%)_____

Shipping Charge (See below)_____

Total Amount Enclosed_____

Please allow 6 - 8 weeks for delivery.
Thank you for your order.

U. S. Funds Only. Please
Please write your check or money order
to Union of Tao and Man

Shipping Charge - All Orders Sent Via U.S. Postal Service, unless specified.
Domestic Surface Mail: First item $2.00, each additional, add $.50.
Canada/Mexico Surface Mail: First item $2.50, each additional, add $1.00.
Other Foreign Surface Mail: First Item $3.00, each additional, add $2.00.
Foreign Air Mail: First item $18.00, each additional, add $7.00.

Credit Card orders only: **VISA** ☐ Visa   **MasterCard** ☐ MasterCard
(13 or 16 digits)   (16 digits)

Card Account Number: | | | | | | | | | | | | | | | | |
1 2 3 4 5 6 7 8 9 10 11 12 13 14 15 16

Expiration Date of Card [ ] — [ ]

Signature:_____

Spiritual Study Through the College of Tao

The College of Tao and the Union of Tao and Man were established formally in California in the 1970's. This tradition is a very old spiritual culture of mankind, holding long experience of human spiritual growth. Its central goal is to offer healthy spiritual education to all people of our society. This time tested tradition values the spiritual development of each individual self and passes down its guidance and experience.

Master Ni carries his tradition from its country of origin to the west. He chooses to avoid making the mistake of old-style religions that have rigid establishments which resulted in fossilizing the delicacy of spiritual reality. Rather, he prefers to guide the teachings of his tradition as a school of no boundary rather than a religion with rigidity. Thus, the branches or centers of this Taoist school offer different programs of similar purpose. Each center extends its independent service, but all are unified in adopting Master Ni's work as the foundation of teaching to fulfill the mission of providing spiritual education to all people.

The centers offer their classes, teaching, guidance and practices on building the groundwork for cultivating a spiritually centered and well-balanced life. As a person obtains the correct knowledge with which to properly guide himself or herself, he or she can then become more skillful in handling the experiences of daily life. The assimilation of good guidance in one's practical life brings about different stages of spiritual development.

Any interested individual is welcome to join and learn to grow for oneself. You might like to join the center near where you live, or you yourself may be interested in organizing a center or study group based on the model of existing centers. In that way, we all work together for the spiritual benefit of all people. We do not require any religious type of commitment.

The learning is life. The development is yours. The connection of study may be helpful, useful and serviceable, directly to you.

- -

Mail to: Union of Tao and Man, 117 Stonehaven Way, Los Angeles, CA 90049

_____ I wish to be put on the mailing list of the Union of Tao and Man to be notified of classes, educational activities and new publications.

Name:_____

Address:_____

City:_____State:_____Zip:_____

Herbs Used by Ancient Taoist Masters

The pursuit of everlasting youth or immortality throughout human history is an innate human desire. Long ago, Chinese esoteric Taoists went to the high mountains to contemplated nature, strengthen their bodies, empower their minds and develop their spirit. From their studies and cultivation, they gave China alchemy and chemistry, herbology and acupuncture, the I Ching, astrology, martial arts and T'ai Chi Chuan, Chi Gong and many other useful kinds of knowledge.

Most important, they handed down in secrecy methods for attaining longevity and spiritual immortality. There were different levels of approach; one was to use a collection of food herb formulas that were only available to highly achieved Taoist masters. They used these food herbs to increase energy and heighten vitality. This treasured collection of herbal formulas remained within the Ni family for centuries.

Now, through Traditions of Tao, the Ni family makes these foods available for you to use to assist the foundation of your own positive development. It is only with a strong foundation that expected results are produced from diligent cultivation.

As a further benefit, in concert with the Taoist principle of self-sufficiency, Traditions of Tao offers the food herbs along with the Union of Tao and Man's publications in a distribution opportunity for anyone serious about financial independence.

Send to: *Traditions of Tao*
                 c/o 117 Stonehaven Way
                 Los Angeles, CA 90049

☐ *Please send me a Traditions of Tao brochure.*

☐ *Please send me information on becoming an independent distributor of Traditions of Tao herbal products and publications.*

Name _____

Address _____

City _____*State* _____*Zip* _____

Phone (day) _____*(night)* _____

Yo San University of Traditional Chinese Medicine
"Not just a medical career, but a life-time commitment to raising one's spiritual standard."

Thank you for your support and interest in our publications and services. It is by your patronage that we continue to offer you the practical knowledge and wisdom from this venerable Taoist tradition.

Because of your sustained interest in Taoism, we formed Yo San University of Traditional Chinese Medicine, a non-profit educational institute in January 1989 under the direction of founder Master Ni, Hua-Ching. Yo San University is the continuation of 38 generations of Ni family practitioners who handed down knowledge and wisdom from fathers to sons. Its purpose is to train and graduate practitioners of the highest caliber in Traditional Chinese Medicine, which includes acupuncture, herbology and spiritual development.

We view Traditional Chinese Medicine as the application of spiritual development. Its foundation is the spiritual capability to know life, to know a person's problem and how to cure it. We teach students how to care for themselves and others, and emphasize the integration of traditional knowledge and modern science. We offer a complete Master's degree program approved by the California State Department of Education that provides an excellent education in Traditional Chinese Medicine and meets all requirements for state licensure.

We invite you to inquire into our school about a creative and rewarding career as a holistic physician. Classes are also open to persons interested only in self-enrichment. For more information, please fill out the form below and send it to:

Yo San University,
12304 Santa Monica Blvd. Suite 104,
Los Angeles, CA 90025

☐ Please send me information on the Masters degree program in Traditional Chinese Medicine.

☐ Please send me information on health workshops and seminars.

☐ Please send me information on continuing education for acupuncturists and health professionals.

Name _____

Address_____

City_____State_____Zip_____

Phone(day)_____(night)_____